Gordon College 8/82

W9-BWA-801

DOING WELL IN COLLEGE
A Concise Guide
to Reading, Writing, and Study Skills

DOING WELL IN

John Langan
Atlantic Community College

Judith Nadell
Glassboro State College

COLLEGE

*A Concise Guide
to Reading, Writing,
and Study Skills*

McGraw-Hill Book Company
New York   St. Louis   San Francisco
Auckland   Bogotá
Hamburg   Johannesburg   London
Madrid   Mexico   Montreal
New Delhi   Panama
Paris   São Paulo   Singapore
Sydney   Tokyo   Toronto

For Our Parents

DOING WELL IN COLLEGE
A Concise Guide to Reading, Writing,
and Study Skills

Copyright © 1980 by McGraw-Hill, Inc. All rights
reserved. Printed in the United States of America.
No part of this publication may be reproduced, stored
in a retrieval system, or transmitted, in any form or
by any means, electronic, mechanical, photocopying,
recording, or otherwise, without the prior written
permission of the publisher.

234567890   DODO   89876543210

This book was set in Century Schoolbook by
Monotype Composition Company, Inc. The editor
was William A. Talkington; the designer was Merrill
Haber; the production supervisor was Richard A.
Ausburn.
R. R. Donnelley & Sons Company was printer and
binder.

See Acknowledgments on page 196. Copyrights
included on this page by reference.

Library of Congress Cataloging in Publication Data

Langan, John,   date
    Doing well in college.

    Includes index.
    1. Study, Method of.   2.   Report writing.
3.   Developmental reading.   4.   English language—
Rhetoric.   I.   Nadell, Judith, joint author.   II.   Title.
LB2395.L34   378.1'7'02812   79-23014
ISBN 0-07-036262-9

Contents

Preface

Doing Well in College is a highly practical guide. Its twelve compact chapters describe the key reading, writing, and study skills you need for success in college. At the end of each chapter is a series of activities to help you master the skills and make them habits. In addition to its nuts-and-bolts approach, *Doing Well in College* has other important features:

- It is complete. It contains the central skills needed to become an effective student. It was written in response to a question that many teachers and students ask: What are the essential skills a person really needs to know to do well in college?

- It is realistic. *Doing Well in College* uses material taken from a variety of college textbooks and gives practice in common study situations. The book grows out of our work not only with students but also with a wide range of teachers who are concerned about developing their students' reading, writing, and study skills. All the skills and activities in the book have been classroom-tested and have been found to get results.

- It presents skills as processes which can be mastered in a step-by-step sequence. Almost every skill is made up of a series of smaller skills or steps. Each step is clearly explained, and practice is often given in the separate steps as well as in the entire skill.

- It is flexible. Each of the twelve chapters is self-contained and deals with a specific area, making it easy for you to turn quickly to the skill you want to work on. At the same time, cross references show how the skills relate to and reinforce one another.

- It is highly adaptable. The book may be used as a core text in a study skills course, as a supplement to another college course, as a guide during college orientation, or in a lab setting. *Doing Well in College* is equally valuable for the individual reader who picks it up, hoping it will deliver the promise of its title.

- It has an easy-to-follow, conversational style and contains especially interesting materials. For example, selections on shyness, ecology, medical confidentiality, and common defense mechanisms are used to illustrate key skills. We believe that skills are mastered more readily when practice materials are engaging and when explanations are friendly and helpful.

- It describes skills in roughly the sequence in which you will need them. The introductory chapter, "Doing Well in College," helps you analyze your attitude about being in college and offers suggestions about how to get off to a strong start. Since you may be taking other courses at the same time you are using this book, you might next read "Taking and Studying Classroom Notes," which shows how to take effective notes in all your classes and how to study them. Early in the semester, you'll want to work through the section on "Managing Your Time." There you will learn how to use your time efficiently and to develop consistent study habits. When you begin to get textbook assignments, study the skills presented in the two chapters on "Reading and Studying Textbooks." You might then go on to "Training Your Memory," because that chapter presents techniques to help you remember classroom and textbook notes. As exams approach, read "Taking Objective and Essay Exams," which shows how to prepare for both kinds of exams and explains test-taking techniques. When your instructors begin assigning papers, be sure to read "Writing Effective Papers," which presents the specific steps you should take to do solid written work. Similarly, the chapters "Doing a Summary" and "Preparing a Report" offer helpful suggestions about how to prepare these two common assignments. And last, "Using the Library" and "Writing the Research Paper" will provide valuable help for research projects.

In short, *Doing Well in College* will help you become an independent learner—a person who can take on the challenge of any college course. What remains, however, is your personal determination to do the work needed to become a successful student. If you decide—and only you can decide—that you want to make your college years productive and worthwhile, this book will help you reach that goal.

John Langan
Judith Nadell

1

Doing Well in College

This chapter will help you:

- Examine your attitude about being in college
- Get a good schedule of courses
- Learn the ground rules for each course
- Keep up with your courses
- Think about long-term goals

If you asked a cross section of students why they are in college, you would probably get a wide range of responses. People go to college to educate and enrich themselves, to prepare for a specific career, to please their friends or family, and for a number of other reasons. Whatever the reasons, just about everyone hopes college will be a positive, worthwhile experience. Few if any students set out intending to waste their college years.

As college teachers, both of us meet students who don't consciously plan to wreck their chances in school and yet end up doing exactly that. Such students come to feel that they *can't* do the work required. But often their real problem is they *don't know how* to do the work. This book will help you develop the key skills needed to handle the academic demands of college life. Specifically, the book describes the reading, study, and writing skills you need to do well in your courses. Having these skills will enable you to take the fullest possible advantage of all that college has to offer.

As important as skills are, something else is even more important: your *attitude* about being in school. Without the right frame of mind, you are not likely to do well in college.

HAVING THE RIGHT ATTITUDE

Your attitude must say, "I will do the work." The two of us meet 400 or so students each year. At first we cannot tell which students have this attitude and which do not. Some time must pass. As the semester unfolds, classes must be attended and assignments must get done. The crunch comes, and the crunch is the plain, hard work that college requires. Some people take on the work and persist even if they hit snags and problems; others don't take on the work or don't persist when things get rough. Then it becomes clear which students have determined, "I will do the work." This inner commitment to getting the work done is probably the single most important factor needed for success in college.

Doing the Work Despite Difficulties

Some people joke that college orientation—the day or so before the start of the first semester—lasts a year or more for many students. The joke is all too often true. Students may find that the first year of college is a time of unsettling change and adjustment. They may start questioning long-accepted personal values. They often begin thinking about career goals. They are in a new environment and must learn to form new relationships. If they have been away from school for several years, or were never serious students in high school, they may have to spend a good deal of time developing effective study habits. In addition, they may find that existing financial, personal, or family problems create even more stress during this already anxious period in their lives. For these and other reasons, we have seen many students go through very rough adjustment periods in their first year of college.

Invariably, the students who succeed, despite their difficulties, have determined to do the work. You too, despite the worries and demands you may experience during a semester, must resolve to get the work done. Otherwise you will lose valuable opportunities that may not come your way again.

Rather than trying to do the work, you may decide to drop a course or drop out of college for a semester. Your decision may be exactly the right thing to do, but before taking such an important step, be sure to talk to someone about your plans. At school you will find people to talk to—counselors, advisers, teachers, and others—who can help you get a perspective on your situation. From time to time, all of us need the insights into ourselves that we cannot possibly get alone but that other people can offer us.

Avoiding the Work

As the semester progresses and the work pressure builds, students must make a choice. They have two alternatives. One is to do the work: to leave the game table, click off the stereo or television, turn down the invition to go out, and go off alone to get the work done. The other alternative is to avoid the work, and there are countless ways to do this.

We have described below some of the tactics students use to avoid studying. If you see yourself in any of these situations, you should do some serious thinking about whether now is the right time for you to be in college. If you are unsure of your commitment, don't coast along, trying to ignore the situation. Instead, make an appointment with a counselor, your academic adviser, or some other interested person. That way you will confront your problem and begin to deal with it.

"I Can't Do It"

Both of us have known students who adopt a defeatist attitude from the very start. Convinced they cannot do the work, they don't even try. However, the only way students can find out whether or not they can do something is by trying—giving it their best shot. Most colleges will give determined students plenty of help by making available such services as tutoring programs and reading, writing, and math labs.

"I'm Too Busy"

Some students make themselves too busy, taking on a job that is not absolutely necessary or working more hours on a job than they need to. Others get overly involved in social activities on and off campus. Still others make personal or family problems so tangled and pressing that they cannot concentrate on their work. There are real cases where people become so busy or troubled that they cannot do their work. But there are many cases where students unconsciously create conflicts so that they have an excuse for not doing what they know they should.

"I'm Too Tired"

We've heard students say that they become tired as soon as it's time to write a paper, study a book, or go to class. Then their weariness clears up when the pressure is off. This "sleepiness syndrome" also expresses itself in the imagined need for naps during the day and ten hours or more of sleep at night. Such students are, often literally, closing their minds to the hard work that college demands.

"I'll Do It Later"

Everyone tends at times to procrastinate—to put things off. Some students, however, constantly postpone doing assignments and setting aside regular study hours. Time and time again they put off what needs to be done so they can watch TV, talk to a friend, go to the movies, play cards, or do any one of a hundred other things. These students typically wind up cramming for tests and writing last-minute papers. Yet they often seem surprised and angry at the low grades they receive.

"I'm Bored with the Subject"

Students sometimes explain that they are doing poorly in a course because the instructor or the subject matter is boring. These students want education to be high-pitch entertainment—an unrealistic expectation. On the whole, college courses and instructors balance out: some will be boring, some will be exciting, many will be somewhere in between. If a course is not interesting, students should be all the more motivated to do the work so they can leave the course behind once and for all.

"I'm Here and That's What Counts"

Some people spend a good part of college lost in a dangerous fantasy. They feel, "Everything will be fine. I am here in college. I have a student I.D. card in my wallet, a parking sticker on the bumper of my car, and textbooks under my arm. All this proves I am a college student. I have it made." Such students have succumbed to a fantasy we all indulge in at times: the belief that we will get something for nothing. But everyone knows from experience that such a hope is false. Life seldom gives us something for nothing—and college won't either. To get somewhere and to become someone, we must be prepared to make a solid effort. By making such a decision and acting on it, we assume control of our lives.

GETTING OFF TO A STRONG START

Having a Good Schedule

Getting a good schedule is one way to start out well in college. Many schools require that all students have a fixed schedule their first semester. However, if you have some choice about what courses to take, make sure you read your college catalog closely. It may describe the content and objectives of most courses and indicate *prerequisites*— other courses or experiences you must have before enrolling. If you don't have the stated prerequisites, do not sign up for a course.

Before making up your schedule, it's a good idea to speak to some knowledgeable people who can help you select interesting and appropriate courses. Academic advisors, counselors, or upper-level students can give you sound advice about scheduling.

Try to plan your classes so you don't schedule on one day an uninterrupted series of lectures or labs. Such a routine can be fatiguing and prevent you from doing your best work.

Every year we come across students who take on more than they can handle. They end up with a heavy schedule and an impossible workload. You shouldn't, then, schedule more than the recommended number of courses your first semester. Also, if you hold down a job while going to school, you might want to adjust your schedule so you don't take a full course load the first semester. If you find you have the time and energy to take on more school work, add an extra course or two to your schedule in later semesters.

Learning the Ground Rules for Each Course

Another way to make a good start is to learn the ground rules for each of your courses. Many instructors explain course requirements in the first class, so be sure you're there and take notes. Your instructors may also distribute a *syllabus* or course description. Look at the syllabus carefully. It often tells where the instructor's office is, lists the instructor's office hours, and presents information about attendance, quizzes and exams, required reading, and so on. If such information is not covered in the syllabus or by the instructor, be sure to ask your instructor about these matters.

If you feel, after hearing the instructor's introductory comments and reading the syllabus, that you cannot meet the course requirements, you may want to consider dropping the course and adding another in its place. (Most schools have a drop-add period during the first week or so of the semester.) Don't feel uncomfortable about dropping a course as long as you have a strong reason. It will do you no good to suffer through a course you are not yet equipped to handle.

The first week or so of a new semester is generally hectic. If there are mix-ups in your schedule and you can't make it to the first or second class, let the instructor know that you haven't dropped the course and that you plan to attend class regularly. Also, don't forget to get the course syllabus and check with the instructor—not other students—about any work assigned during the classes you missed.

Keeping Up with Your Courses

If you have problems understanding the material in a course, don't waste time complaining about the subject or the instructor. And don't sit back calmly and assume that everything will work out. Make sure you get help, either from another student or from your instructor. Many students are reluctant to go to their instructors for help, but that is why teachers have office hours. Take advantage of these set-aside times.

Whenever you are absent, you should ask the instructor, not other students, about missed assignments. It's wise not to rely on other students for this information because they may not have understood the assignment or may not explain it to you clearly. Your work will invariably reflect this confusion. By going to your instructor, you will not only get your information firsthand but you will demonstrate your commitment to your work.

THINKING ABOUT LONG-TERM GOALS

Some students have trouble doing well in college because they have little idea why they are in school and little sense of what they would like to do after graduation. Such students settle on their majors haphazardly and take courses at random. Not surprisingly, these students often have trouble motivating themselves to do college work.

To avoid this trap, it's important that you take some time early in college to ask yourselves some hard questions: Why are you in college? What do you hope to get from your college education? What are your long-term goals? What steps do you plan to take to reach those long-term goals? Your answers to these questions can give direction to your college years and motivate you to do the hard work needed to succeed.

During your first year, plan to visit the college's counseling center. The center probably administers an *interest inventory* and a *vocational preference test*. The first identifies what you like and can do well; the second points to careers that match your interests and abilities. With this information, the counseling staff at the center can help you decide on a suitable academic major.

Some time early in college, you should make an appointment to talk with a faculty member in the department of your intended major. Most departments have advisers who set aside time to meet with students and discuss their course of study. From these advisers, you can learn many things: what courses are required, which are recommended, and what field or training experiences are available. Having this information is essential if you want a sound and rewarding academic program.

Also, some time during your first year, plan to go to the placement office to get specific information on careers. Many students have the mistaken notion that placement offices provide career information only to about-to-graduate students. Such is not the case. It is very important for beginning students to speak to the placement staff to obtain updated information about the future of specific fields. For example, it would make little sense for you to plan to become a history teacher if that particular job market will have few openings at the time you graduate.

In short, you should try—early in college—to do some serious thinking about who you are, where you are going, and how you will get there. Then you can set some personally meaningful goals that will motivate you to do your best.

A final note is in order. We are not suggesting that college courses are meaningful only if they prepare you for the work you plan to do after graduation. You don't want to limit yourself only to those courses you will use in a practical way. College is the perfect time to explore new areas of knowledge—without being concerned whether or not the material has practical value. Also, we are not implying that you must, early in college, make a final decision about what you want to do and then limit yourself to a single course of action. Such an approach would restrict your opportunities to learn and grow. Remember that one of the most exciting things about life is that you, like other people, are constantly changing and gaining new insights into your interests, abilities, and goals. Still, by beginning to think—as early as you can—about your long-term goals and about what you can do to reach them, you are bound to commit yourself more seriously to your work. In other words, you will be on your way to doing well in college.

Activities

1 Review the chapter carefully. Then, without looking back, answer the following questions.

1. Probably the single most important thing you must do to succeed in college is:
   a. Understand avoidance tactics.
   b. Get a reasonable schedule.
   c. Think about long-term goals.
   d. Have the right attitude.

2. True or false: _____ Prerequisites are the objectives and assignments for a course.

3. If you find yourself in a boring course, which of the following should you do:
   a. Attend class only when necessary.
   b. Drop the course.
   c. Work hard so you can get the course behind you.
   d. None of the above.

4. List three tactics some students use to avoid doing the work required in college:

   a. _____

   b. _____

   c. _____

5. True or false: _____ You should try to schedule all your lecture classes on one day of the week.

6. To get information on scheduling, you should do which of the following:
   a. Speak to your adviser.
   b. Consult the college catalog.
   c. Talk to upper-level students.
   d. All of the above.

7. Where can you go on campus to get specific information about careers? _____

8. The course syllabus often provides information on which of the following:
   a. The instructor's attendance policy
   b. The number of quizzes and exams
   c. The amount of reading required
   d. All of the above

9. The _____ administers an interest inventory and a vocational preference test.

10. True or false: _____ You should take courses only if they prepare you for the job you would like to have after graduation.

2 Evaluate your commitment to serious study by noting how often you use each of the avoidance tactics listed below.

1. "I can't do it."
   I use this excuse: ____often ____sometimes ____rarely ____never

2. "I'm too busy."
   I use this excuse: ____often ____sometimes ____rarely ____never

3. "I'm too tired."
   I use this excuse: ____often ____sometimes ____rarely ____never

4. "I'll do it later."
   I use this excuse: ____often ____sometimes ____rarely ____never

5. "I'm bored with the subject."
   I use this excuse: ____often ____sometimes ____rarely ____never

6. "I'm here and that's what counts."
   I use this excuse: ____often ____sometimes ____rarely ____never

2

Managing Your Time

This chapter will show you how to manage your time
through the use of:

- A large monthly calendar

- A weekly study schedule

- A "To Do" list

All of us need free time, hours without demands and obligations, so we can just relax and do what we please. But it is easy to lose track of time and discover suddenly that there aren't enough hours to do what needs to be done. No skill is more basic to survival in college than time control. If you do not use your time well, your college career—and the life goals that depend on how well you do in college—will slip like sand through your fingers. This chapter describes three methods to help you gain control of your time: you will learn how to use a large monthly calendar, a weekly study schedule, and a daily or weekly "To Do" list.

A LARGE MONTHLY CALENDAR

You should buy or make a large monthly calendar. Such a calendar is your first method of time control because it allows you, in one quick glance, to get a clear picture of what you need to do in the weeks to come. Be sure your monthly calendar has a good-sized block of white space for each date. Then, as soon as you learn about exam dates and paper deadlines, enter them clearly in the appropriate spot on the calendar. Hang the calendar in a place where you will see it every day, perhaps on your kitchen or bedroom wall.

In the spaces below write the names of the courses you are taking. Also, record the dates on which papers or other assignments are due and the dates on which exams are scheduled. Due dates are often listed in a course syllabus as well as announced by a course instructor.

Courses	Paper Due Dates	Exam Dates
_____	_____	_____
_____	_____	_____
_____	_____	_____
_____	_____	_____
_____	_____	_____

Transfer all this information to a monthly calendar.

- Write here the best place for you to post a monthly calendar:
  _____.

A WEEKLY STUDY SCHEDULE

A weekly study schedule will make you aware of how much time you actually have each week and will help you use that time effectively.

Look over the master weekly schedule (page 14) which one student, Rich, prepared to gain control of his time. Then read carefully the points that follow; all are important in planning an effective weekly schedule.

Important Points about a Weekly Study Schedule

1   **Plan, at first, at least one hour of study time for each hour of class time.**   Depending on the course, the grade you want, and your own study efficiency, you may have to schedule more time later. A difficult course, for example, may require three hours or more of study time for each course hour. Remember that learning is what counts, not the time it takes you to learn. Be prepared to schedule as much time as you need to gain control of a course.

   • How many class hours, excluding Lab and Physical Education, does Rich have?   _____

   • How many study hours has he scheduled?   _____

2   **Schedule regular study time.**   To succeed in your college work, you need to establish definite study hours. If you do not set aside and stick to such hours on a daily or almost daily basis, you are probably going to fail at time control. Take a minute or two to jot down in the spaces below the free hours each day that you would use as regular study time. As an example, the first column shows Rich's free hours on Monday.

| For Rich | Your Possible Study Hours | | | | | | |
Mon.	Mon.	Tues.	Wed.	Thurs.	Fri.	Sat.	Sun.
9-10	___	___	___	___	___	___	___
2-4	___	___	___	___	___	___	___
___	___	___	___	___	___	___	___

There are many values to setting aside regular study hours. First of all, they help make studying a habit. Study times will be as automatically programmed into your daily schedule as, say, watching a favorite television program. You will not have to remind yourself to study, nor will you waste large amounts of time and energy trying to avoid studying; you will simply do it. Another value of regular study time is that you will be better able to stay up to date on work in your courses. You are not likely to find yourself several days before a test with three textbook chapters to read or five weeks of classroom notes to organize and study. Finally,

RICH'S SCHEDULE

	MON.	TUES.	WED.	THURS.	FRI.	SAT.	SUN.
6:00 a.m.							
7:00	B		B		B		
8:00	Eng.	B	Eng.		Eng.	B	
9:00	▓	▓		B	▓		B
10:00	Psy	Phy Ed	Psy	▓	Psy	Job	
11:00	↓			▓		↓	▓
12:00	L	L		L	L		
1:00 p.m.	Bio	Lab	Bio	▓	Bio		L
2:00	▓		↓	▓			
3:00	▓	↓	Job		Job		
4:00			↓	▓			
5:00	S	S	↓	S		↓	S
6:00				S		S	
7:00	Speech	▓		Soc	↓		▓
8:00		▓	▓	↓	S		▓
9:00	↓		▓	↓			▓
10:00		▓					
11:00							
12:00							
1:00	③	④	③	⑤	②	⓪	⑤

B = Breakfast	▓ = Study blocks	Psy = Psychology	Eng = English
L = Lunch	O = Study hours per day	Soc = Sociology	Phy Ed = Physical
S = Supper	Blanks = Free time	Bio = Biology	Education

regular study takes advantage of the proven fact that a series of study sessions is more effective for learning material than a single long "cram" session.

- How many separate blocks of study time has Rich built into his weekly schedule? _____

- How many benefits of regular study hours are described in the preceding paragraph? (*Hint:* Word signals such as "First of all" are clues to each separate value.) _____

3 **Plan at least one-hour blocks of study time.** If you schedule less than one hour, your study period may be over just when you are fully warmed up and working hard.

- What is the largest single block of study time that Rich has during the week? (Write down the day and the number of hours.)

  _____

- What is the largest single block of study time available to you each week? _____

4 **Reward yourself for using study time effectively.** Research shows that people work better if they get an immediate reward for their efforts. So if your schedule permits, try to set up a reward system. Allow yourself to telephone a friend or watch a television show or eat a snack after a period of efficient study. On Rich's schedule, for example, 9:00 to 10:00 on Tuesday night is free for watching television as a reward for working well in the hour-and-a-half study slot before. When you are studying over a several-hour period, you can also give yourself "mini-rewards" of five to ten minutes of free time for every hour or so of study time.

  Your reward system won't work if you "cheat," so deprive yourself of such pleasures as television shows when you have not studied honestly.

- Locate the other spots where Rich has built reward time into his schedule after study periods and indicate the hours here: _____

  _____

- Do you think it is a good idea for Rich to reward himself with one day in the week (Saturday) free from study? Why or why not? _____

5 **Try to schedule study periods before and after classes.** Ideally, you should read a textbook chapter before a teacher covers it; what you hear in class will then be a "second exposure," and so the ideas are likely to be a good deal more meaningful to you. You should also look over your notes from the preceding class in case the teacher discusses the material further. Similarly, if you take a few minutes to review your notes as soon after class as possible, you will be able to organize and clarify the material while it is still fresh in your mind.

- If a new textbook chapter were to be covered in Rich's sociology class on Thursday, where in his schedule should he plan to read it? _____

6 **Work on your most difficult subjects when you are most alert.** Save routine work for times you are most likely to be tired. You might, for example, study a new and difficult math chapter at 8 p.m. if you are naturally alert then and review vocabulary words for a Spanish class at 11 p.m., when you may be a little tired.

- Assuming that Rich is most naturally alert early in the day and that biology is his most difficult subject, in what time slots should he schedule his work on that subject? _____
- At what time of day do you consider yourself most alert? _____

7 **Balance your activities.** Allow free time for family, friends, sports, television, and so on in your schedule. Note that there is a good deal of free time (empty space) in Rich's schedule, even with his classes, work, and study hours.

- Where is the biggest block of free time in Rich's schedule? _____

- Where do you plan to have a substantial block of free time?

8 **Keep your schedule flexible.** When unexpected events occur, trade times on your weekly timetable. Do not simply do away with study hours. If you find that your schedule requires constant adjustments, revise it. (Your instructor may be able to give you extra copies of the schedule on page 17.) After two or three revisions, you will have a realistic, practical weekly schedule that you can follow honestly.

- If Rich went to a family reunion on Sunday at 1 p.m. and didn't get back until 8:00 that evening, where in his schedule could he make up at least some of the missed hours of study time? _____

- Keeping the above points in mind, use the form on page 17 to make up your own realistic weekly study schedule. Write in your class and lab periods first; next add in your hours for job and meals; and then fill in the study hours that you need to do well in your courses. At the bottom of your schedule, make up a key that explains the symbols you have used in the schedule. Also add up and circle the total number of study hours you realistically plan to set aside each day.

YOUR SCHEDULE

	Mon.	Tues.	Wed.	Thurs.	Fri.	Sat.	Sun.
6 a.m.							
7							
8							
9							
10							
11							
12							
1 p.m.							
2							
3							
4							
5							
6							
7							
8							
9							
10							
11							
12							
1 a.m.							

Other Study Hints

Here are three additional study hints that you should keep in mind.

1 **If possible, study in a well-lighted place where you can sit comfortably and be quiet and alone.**
    a. To avoid glare, make sure that light comes from above or over your shoulder, not from in front of you. Also, you should have more than one light source in the room. For example, you might use a ceiling light in addition to a pole lamp behind your chair.

b. Do not try to study in a completely relaxed position. A light muscular tension promotes the concentration needed for study. So sit on an upright chair, or sit in a cross-legged position on your bed with a pillow behind you.

c. To mask distracting noises that come from outside your room (people talking or walking about, the sound of a television, street noise, and so on), you may want to create a steady background sound. This might be a fan, an air conditioner, or a stereo or radio playing soft, soothing music.

d. To avoid interruptions, ask your family and friends to please keep away during study hours. Tell them that you will return telephone calls after you finish studying.

If you do not have a room where you can study, use a secluded spot in the library or student center or find some other quiet spot where you can work. If you have one particular place where you usually do most of your studying, you will almost automatically shift into gear and begin studying when you go to that place.

2   **Stay in good physical condition.**   You do not want to be prey to quick fatigue or frequent bouts of sickness. Eat nourishing meals; you will probably master a difficult psychology chapter more easily if you have had a solid breakfast than if you had only a cup of coffee. Try to get an average of eight hours of sleep a night unless your system can manage with less. Also, try to exercise on a regular basis. A short workout in the morning (if only five minutes of running in place) will help sustain your energy flow during the day. Finally, do not hesitate to take a fifteen- to thirty-minute nap at some point during the day. Research findings show that such a nap can provide a helpful energy boost.

3   **Use outside study help when needed.**   Some people find studying with a friend or friends genuinely helpful. Others, however, find it more of a distraction than an aid because they spend more time chatting than studying cooperatively. Use the technique of team study when you think it will be of real value to you. Also, find out if your school or individual departments have a tutoring service. If so, do not hesitate to use the service to get help on a particular subject or subjects. Having a good tutor could make a significant difference in your grade for a course. Determine if your school, like many, has a learning center where you may work on developing writing, reading, study, and math skills. Finally, learn the office hours of your professors and find out whether you can see them if you need additional help.

A DAILY OR WEEKLY "TO DO" LIST

A "To Do" list is simply a list of things a person wants to accomplish within a limited period of time. Many successful people make the "To Do" list a habit, considering it an essential step in making the most efficient use of their time each day. A "To Do" list, made up daily or weekly, may be one of the most important single study habits you will ever acquire.

Prepare your "To Do" list on 4×6 inch notepads or in a small notebook. (Such a notebook can also be used to record the daily assignments you receive in your different courses.) A weekly list is usually prepared on a Sunday for the week ahead; a daily list is prepared the evening before a new day or the first thing on the morning of that day. The list should include all the things you want to work on during that week or day.

Below is Rich's "To Do" list for one day.

RICH'S "TO DO" LIST

```
  To Do                                        Monday

 * 1 Proofread English paper before class
   2 Read Chap. 4 of Psychology text
 * 3 Memorize study notes for Bio. test on Wednesday
 * 4 Coordinate class Bio. note with Chap. 3 of the text
   5 Buy jeans during sale at K-Mart
 * 6 Rehearse 2-minute speech for tonight's class
   7 Fix slipcovers on car
   8 Wash car
   9 Borrow Billy Joel albums from Al
  10 Call Sue sometime
  11 Borrow + copy notes from Psy. class missed last week
  12 Monday night football!
 *13 Review Bio. notes 1/2 hour before bed
```

Important Notes about the "To Do" List

1 **Carry the list with you throughout the day.**   A small notebook can be kept in a purse and a 4×6 inch slip of paper can be kept in a pocket or wallet.

2 **Decide priorities.**   Making the best use of your time means focusing on top-priority items rather than spending hours completing low-priority activities. When in doubt about what to do at any given time in the day, ask yourself, "How can I best use my time at this point?" Many people place an asterisk (*) in front of the high-priority items on their list.

3 **Cross out items as you finish them.**   Don't worry unnecessarily about completing your list; what is not done can probably be moved onto the next day's list. What is important is that you make the best possible use of your time each day. Focus on top-priority activities!

• On a separate sheet of paper, make up your own "To Do" list for tomorrow. Put an asterisk in front of high-priority items.

Final Thoughts

You now have several practical means of gaining control of your time: a monthly calendar, a master study schedule, and a "To Do" list. Use whatever combination of the techniques is best for you. These tools, combined with your own determination to apply them, can reduce the disorder of everyday life, where time all too often slips quickly and silently away. Through time planning, you can achieve the consistency in your work that is absolutely vital for success in school. And through time control, you can take command of your life and accomplish more work than you ever have before.

Activities

1 Evaluate your time control skills and study habits by putting a check mark beside each of the skills or habits that you already practice. Then put a check mark beside those steps that you plan to practice. Leave a space blank if you do not plan to follow a particular strategy.

	Now Do	Plan to Do
• Use a large monthly calendar.		
• Use a weekly study schedule.		
• Use a daily or weekly "To Do" List.		
• Have regular study hours.		
• Schedule as many hours as needed for a particular course.		
• Have rewards for using study time effectively.		
• Work on difficult subjects at times when most alert.		
• Balance activities.		
• Reschedule study times when regular study hours are interrupted.		
• Study in a well-lighted, comfortable, quiet place.		
• Stay in good physical condition.		
• Use outside study help when needed.		

2 Review the chapter carefully. Then, without looking back, answer the following questions.

   1. What dates should you mark off on a large monthly calendar?

   _____

   2. What are the three principal steps that you should take to gain control of your time?

   a. Watch your health.
   b. Use a daily or weekly "To Do" list.
   c. Study every day of the week.
   d. Use a large monthly calendar.
   e. Keep your schedule flexible.
   f. Make up a weekly study schedule.

3. You can probably study most effectively in a:
   a. Very tense position
   b. Slightly tense position
   c. Completely relaxed position

4. The value of regular study hours is:
   a. You will make studying a habit.
   b. You will stay up to date on courses.
   c. You will learn more effectively by spacing your study sessions.
   d. All of the above.

5. When you make up a "To Do" list, you should:
   a. Schedule one-hour blocks of study time.
   b. Mark down exam deadlines.
   c. Decide on priorities.
   d. Hang it on your wall.

3 Read the following description of one student's study situation:

Sally has trouble managing her study time. She claims that the only time she can make herself study is right before a test. "If I'm not in a crisis situation with a test just around the corner," she says, "I usually won't study. When I'm in the right mood, I do try to study a bit to keep things from piling up. But most of the time I'm just not in the mood. Some mornings I get up and say to myself, 'Tonight you will do at least two hours of school work.' Then, 95 percent of the time, I let something distract me." Recently, Sally had to face the shortcomings of her cram study method. She found herself with only one night to prepare for two exams and a report; the result was several disastrous grades.

Now write a one-page (or longer) essay in which you answer *in detail* the question, "What can Sally do to prevent such a situation from happening again?" In your answer, apply the information you have learned in the chapter on time control.

3

Taking and Studying
Classroom Notes

This chapter will show you how to:

- Take effective classroom notes

- Study and remember your notes

If you really want to do well in a course, you must promise yourself that you will go to class faithfully and take good notes. This chapter will offer a series of tips on how to take effective classroom notes. However, the hints will be of no value if you do not attend class. The importance of *regular class attendance* cannot be emphasized enough. Students who cut class rarely do well in college.

The alternatives to class attendance—reading the text or using someone else's notes—can seldom substitute for the experience of being in class and hearing the instructor talk about key ideas in the course. These ideas are often the ones you will be expected to know on exams.

If you do not attend classes regularly, you may be making an unconscious decision that you do not want to attend college at this time. If you think this may be how you feel, talk to a counselor, teacher, or friend. Another person can often help you clarify your own thoughts and feelings so you can achieve a perspective on your situation.

- Have you made a personal decision (be honest!) to attend all your classes regularly? _____
- If not, are you willing to think about why you are reluctant to make the commitment to college work? _____

THIRTEEN HINTS FOR TAKING EFFECTIVE CLASSROOM NOTES

1 **Get down a written record of each class.** It's important that you write down the material covered because forgetting begins almost immediately. Studies have shown that within two weeks you probably will forget 80 percent or more of what you have heard. And in four weeks you are lucky if 5 percent remains! The significance of these facts is so crucial that the point bears repeating: To guard against the relentlessness of forgetting, you must write down much of the information presented in class. Later, you will study your notes so that you understand and re-member the ideas presented in class. And the more complete your notes are when you review them, the more likely you are to master the material.

How many notes should you take? If you pay attention in class, you will soon develop an instinct for what is meaningful and what is not. If you are unsure whether certain terms, facts, and ideas are significant, here is a good rule to follow: When in doubt, write it down. This doesn't mean you should (or could) get down every word, but you should be prepared to do a good deal of writing in class. Also, do not worry if you don't understand everything you record in your notes. Sometimes a teacher will phrase an idea several different ways and it may turn out that it is the third version of the idea that you clearly understand. It is easy to cross out later the material that you don't need but impossible to recover material you never recorded in the first place. Keep in mind that writing too much, rather than too little, may mean the difference between passing and failing a course or between a higher grade and a lower one.

2 **Sit where the teacher will always see you, preferably toward the front of the room.** Your position will help you stay tuned to what the instructor does in class. If you sit behind someone, are hidden in a corner, or are otherwise out of the instructor's line of vision, your attitude may be showing—either you are worried that you may be noticed and called on (a common anxiety) or you don't really want to be there (something worth thinking about).

Analyze your attitude. If you're hiding, know that you're hiding and try to understand why. It is all right not to want to be in a class; teachers can be boring and subjects uninteresting. However, the danger in such cases is that you may slide into a passive state where you won't listen or take notes. Don't fool yourself. If a class is deadly, there is all the more reason to make yourself take good notes—that way you will get out of the class once and for all!

3 **Read in advance about the topic to be discussed in class.** All too often, students don't read assigned textbook material on a topic until after class is over. Lacking the necessary background, they have trouble understanding the new ideas discussed in class. However, if they have made an initial breakthrough on a topic by doing advance reading, they will be able to listen and take notes more easily and with greater understanding. And they should be able to write more organized and effective notes because they will have a general sense of the topic.

Reading the textbook before a lecture is particularly important when the subject is very difficult. You should never attend a lecture in a challenging course without first having read the appropriate textbook material. Reading the text in advance is also helpful if you have spelling problems that hinder notetaking. As you read the text, you should write down recurring terms that may come up in the lecture and that you might have trouble spelling.

4 Record notes as follows:

  a. Use full-sized 8½ × 11 inch paper. Do not use a small tablet. You may need the margin space that comes on a full page; also, on a full page, you are more likely to see groups of related ideas that otherwise might be visually fragmented and not apparent over several small pages.

  b. Keep all the notes from each course together in separate sections of a notebook. Use a loose-leaf notebook sectioned into parts with dividers and index tabs or use a large spiral notebook that has several sections. A loose-leaf book is probably more convenient because it allows you to insert handout sheets and supplementary notes at the appropriate points.

  c. Date each day's notes.

  d. Take notes on one side of the page only and leave space at the top of the page and at the left-hand margin. (You might use notebook paper that has a light red line down the left side.) Using only one side of the paper eliminates the bother, when studying, of having to flip pages over and then flip them back to follow the development of an idea. Having good margins gives you free space to add to your notes if desired. You may, for example, write in ideas taken from your textbook or other sources. Also, the added space can be used to prepare study notes (see page 31) that will help you learn the material.

  e. Write legibly. When you prepare for a test, you want to spend your time studying—not deciphering your handwriting.

  f. Abbreviate recurring terms in order to save time. Put a key for abbreviated words in the top margin of your notes. For example, in a biology class a *ch* could stand for *chromosome;* in a psychology class an *o c* could stand for *operant conditioning.* (When a lecture is over, you may want to go back and fill in the words you have abbreviated.)

  Also abbreviate the following common words, using the symbols shown:

+ = and	def = definition
w/ = with	∴ = therefore
e.g. = for example	info = information
ex = example	1, 2, 3 = one, two, three, etc.

  Note, too, that you can often omit words like *a, and,* and *the.*

  g. Mark off exams or quizzes that are announced as well as assignments that the teacher gives. It's a good idea to circle exam dates and put a large *A* for *Assignment* in the margin. (Be sure you have a definite system for keeping track of assignments. Some students record them in a separate small notepad; others record them at the back of the notebook devoted to a given course.)

5 **Try to write down your notes in the following outline form.** Start main points at the margin. Indent secondary ideas and supporting details. Further indent more subordinate material.

Main points are listed at the margin.
   Secondary points and supporting details are indented.
     More subordinate material is indented further.

Definitions, for instance, should always start at the margin. When a list of terms is presented, the heading should also start at the margin, but each item in the series should be set in slightly from the margin. Examples, too, should be indented under the point they illustrate.

Here is another organizational aid: When the speaker moves from one idea or aspect of a topic to another, show this shift with white space by skipping a line or two.

In the rapid pace of a lecture, you won't always be able to tell what is a main point and what is secondary material. Be ready, though, to use the outline techniques of indention and white space whenever you can. They are the first steps toward organizing class material.

6 **Watch for signals of importance:**
  a. Write down whatever your teacher puts on the board. Put the letters *OB* in the margin to indicate that the material was written on the board. Later, when you review your notes, you will know which ideas the teacher emphasized. The chances are good that they will come up on exams.
  b. Always write down definitions and enumerations. Most people instinctively write down definitions (see page 65) but at times they ignore enumerations. An enumeration is simply a list of items (marked with a 1, 2, 3 or other symbols) that fit under a particular heading. (See also page 66.)

    Teachers use enumerations or lists to show the relationship among a group of ideas. Being aware of enumerations will help you organize material as you take notes. Enumerations are signaled in such ways as: "The four steps in the process are . . ."; "There were three reasons for . . ."; "Five characteristics of . . ."; "The two effects were . . ."; and so on. When you write a list, always mark the items with 1, 2, 3 or other appropriate signals. Also, always be sure to include a clear heading that explains what a list is about. For example, if you list and number six kinds of defense mechanisms, make sure you write at the top of the list the heading, "Kinds of Defense Mechanisms."

c. Your instructor may say, "This is an important reason ..."; or "A point that will keep coming up later ..."; or "The chief cause was ..."; or "The basic idea here is ..."; or "Don't forget that ..."; or "Pay special attention to ..."; and so on. Be sure to write down the important statements announced by these and other emphasis words, and write in the margin *Imp* or some other mark (such as * or ξ) to show their importance.

d. If your teacher repeats a point, you can usually assume it is important. You might write *R* for *Repeated* in the margin so you will know later that your instructor stressed that idea.

e. A teacher's voice may slow down, become louder, or otherwise signal that you are expected to write down exactly what is being said, word for word. Needless to say, do so!

7 **Write down any examples the teacher provides and mark them with *Ex.*** The examples help you understand complex and abstract points. If you don't write examples down, you are likely to forget them later when you need them to make sense of an idea. You may not have to write down every example that illustrates an idea, but you should record at least one example that makes a point clear.

8 **Be sure to write down the details that connect or explain main points.** Too many students copy only the major points the teacher puts on the board. They do not realize that, as time passes, they may forget the specifics which serve as connecting bridges between key ideas. Be sure, then, to record the connecting details the instructor provides. That way you are more apt to remember the relationship among the major points in your notes.

In science and math classes especially, students often fail to record the explanations that make formulas or numerical problems meaningful. Their notes may consist only of the letters and numbers the instructor chalked on the board. But to understand how the letters and numbers are related, they should also write down accompanying explanations and details.

Always take advantage of the connections teachers often make at the beginning or end of a class. They may review material already covered and preview what is to come. Write down such overviews when they are presented and label them *Review* or

Preview, as the case may be. An instructor's summaries or projections will help the course come together for you.

9 **Leave blank spaces for items or ideas you miss.** Right after class, ask another student or the teacher to help you fill in the gaps. Also, if you fall behind in your notetaking, concentrate on getting down what seem to be the main ideas rather than the supporting facts and details. You may be able to get the supporting material later from another student or from your textbook.

10 **Don't hesitate to ask the instructor questions if certain points are confusing to you.** Other students are likely to have the same questions but are reluctant to ask to have the material clarified. Remember that teachers look favorably upon students who show interest and curiosity.

11 **Do not stop taking notes during discussion periods.** Many valuable ideas may come up during informal discussions, ideas that your instructor may not present formally later on.

12 **Do not stop taking notes toward the end of a class.** Because of time spent on discussions, teachers may have to cram important points they want to cover into the last minutes of a class. Be ready to write as rapidly as you can to get down this final rush of ideas.

Be prepared, also, to resist the fatigue that may settle in during class. As a lecture proceeds, the possibility of losing attention increases. You do not want to snap out of a daydream only to realize that an instructor is halfway into an important idea and you haven't even begun writing.

13 **Go over your notes soon after class.** While they are still clear in your mind, make your notes as clear as possible. A day later may be too late because forgetting sets in almost at once.

As far as possible, make sure that punctuation is clear, that unfinished sentences are completed, and that all words are readable and correctly spelled. You may also want to write out completely words that you abbreviated during the lecture. Wherever appropriate, add connecting statements and other comments to clarify the material. Make sure important items such as material on the board, definitions, enumerations, and so on are clearly marked. Improve the organization, if necessary, so that you can see at a glance the differences between main points and supporting material, as well as any relationships among the main points.

STUDYING CLASS NOTES

The best time to start studying your notes is within a day after taking them. Because of the mind's tendency to forget material rapidly, a few minutes of study soon after a class will give you more learning for less time and effort than almost any other technique you will practice.

Study your notes by using the margin space at the side (or top) of each page. Jot down in the margin a series of key words or phrases that will help you pull together and recall the main ideas on the page. Shown on page 31 is a page of notes from a business course. Notice in the side margin the recall words that one student, Janet, used for studying the page of notes.

Turn the recall words in the margin into questions to test yourself on the material. For instance, Janet asked herself, "What is the origin of economics?" After she could recite the answer without looking at it, she asked herself, "What is the definition of economics?" Janet then went back and retested herself on the first question. When she could recite the answers to both the first and second questions, she went on to the third one, "What is an important assumption about economics?" She continued on in this manner, testing herself on each new question and retesting herself on the previous ones, until she could recite all of them from memory. (For more information on repeated self-testing, see page 85.)

This approach, pursued on a regular basis, will help you remember the material covered in your classes. With such a study method, you will not be left with a great deal of material to organize and learn right before an exam. Instead, you will be able to devote preexam time to a final intensive review of the subject.

JANET'S STUDY NOTES

	Business 101 2-7-80 ec = economic(s)
	res = resource
Origin of ec	Economics—from Greek words meaning "HOUSE" and "TO MANAGE." Meaning gradually extended to cover not only management of household but of business and governments.
Def of ec	Ec (definition)—STUDY OF HOW SCARCE RESOURCES ARE ALLOCATED IN A SOCIETY OF UNLIMITED WANTS.
	Every society provides goods + services; these are available in limited quantities and so have value.
Imp assumption	One of most imp. assumptions of ec: Though res of world are limited, wants of people are not. This means an ec system can never produce enough to satisfy everyone completely.
Def of ec res	Ec res—all factors that go into production of
2 types of ec res	goods + services. Two types:
2 kinds of property res + defs	1. PROPERTY RES—2 kinds:
	a. LAND—all natural res (land, timber, water, oil, minerals)
	b. CAPITAL—all the machinery, tools, equipment, + building needed to produce goods + distribute them to consumers.
3 kinds of human res + defs	2. HUMAN RES—3 kinds
	a. LABOR—all physical and mental talents needed to produce goods + services
	b. MANAGERIAL ABILITY—talent needed to bring together land, capital, + labor to produce goods and services.
	c. TECHNOLOGY—accumulated fund of knowledge which helps in production of goods + services.

Activities

1 Evaluate your present notetaking skills by putting a check mark beside each of the thirteen notetaking hints that you already practice. Then put a check mark beside those steps that you plan to practice. Leave a space blank if you do not plan to follow a particular strategy.

	Now Do	Plan to Do
1. Get down a written record of the class.		
2. Sit where the teacher will see you.		
3. Read in advance textbook material about the topic to be presented in class.		
4. Record notes as follows:		
a. Use full-sized 8½ × 11 inch paper.		
b. Use a notebook divided into parts.		
c. Date each day's notes.		
d. Take notes on one side of the page only.		
e. Write legibly.		
f. Abbreviate common words and recurring terms.		
g. Indicate assignments and exams.		
5. Write notes in outline form as follows:		
a. Start main points at the margin; indent secondary points.		
b. Use white space to show shift in thought.		
6. Watch for signals of importance:		
a. Write whatever the teacher puts on the board.		
b. Write definitions and enumerations.		
c. Write down points marked by emphasis words.		
d. Record repeated points.		
e. Note the hints given by the teacher's tone of voice.		
7. Write down examples.		
8. Write down connecting details and explanations.		

9. Do as follows when material is missed:
   a. Leave slots for notes missed.
   b. Try to get the broad sweep of ideas when you fall behind.
10. Question the instructor when an idea isn't clear.
11. Do not stop taking notes during discussion periods.
12. Do not stop taking notes toward the end of a class.
13. Go over your notes soon after class.

Now, evaluate your skills in studying class notes.

- Jot in the margin key words to recall ideas.
- Turn recall words into questions.
- Use repeated self-testing to learn the material.
- Apply this study method regularly.

2 Review the chapter carefully. Then, without looking back, answer the following questions.

1. In only two weeks you may forget up to _____ percent of what you have heard in class. In four weeks you are lucky to remember 5 percent. So to guard against forgetting, it is absolutely essential to _____ the material that you hear in class.

2. Which of the following methods might a teacher use to signal the importance of an idea?
   a. Repetition of a point   d. Enumerations
   b. Emphasis signals   e. All of the above
   c. Tone of voice

3. Often the most important thing you can do to perform well in a course is:
   a. Sit where the instructor can see you and listen carefully.
   b. Write down definitions and examples.
   c. Be in class and take effective notes.
   d. Don't stop taking notes during discussion periods or at the end of a class.

4. Take notes in outline form as far as possible by starting main points at the margin and by _____ secondary points and supporting details. Also, when the speaker moves from one idea or aspect of a topic to another, show this shift by _____ a line or two.

5. True or false: _____ Taking too few rather than too many notes in class is one reason students have trouble doing well in their courses

3 Following are excerpts from notes taken during an introductory lecture in a sociology class. In the margin of the notes, jot down key words or phrases that could be used to pull together and so recall the main ideas on each page.

Sociology 101   1-27-77

In the million years or so of life on earth, human beings have sought truth in many places. FIVE SOURCES OF TRUTH in particular are important to note: (1) intuition, (2) authority, (3) tradition, (4) common sense, and (5) science.

1. INTUITION—any flash of insight (true or mistaken) whose source the receiver cannot fully identify or explain.
    Ex.—Galen in second century made chart of human body showing exactly where it might be pierced without fatal injury. Knew which zones were fatal through intuition.

2. AUTHORITY—persons who are experts in a specific field.

Two kinds of authority:
a. SACRED—rests upon faith that a certain tradition or document—eg., the Bible—is of supernatural origin.

	b. SECULAR—arises from human perception
	+ is of two kinds:
	(1) secular scientific—rests upon empirical
	observation
	(2) secular humanistic—rests upon belief
	that certain "great people" have had
	special insight.
	We must rely on authority in fields outside our
	specialty but also remember that no scientific
	authority has final word on human knowledge.

4 Turn in to your instructor a copy of one day's notes that you have taken in one of your classes. These notes should fill at least one side of a sheet of paper. If you have never taken a full page of notes in class, add a second or third day's notes until you complete at least one sheet. In the top or left-hand margin of your notes, write down key words or phrases you could use to master the material in the notes.

5 The activity that follows will give you practice in taking lecture notes. The activity is based on a short lecture on listening given in a speech class. Take notes on the lecture as your instructor or a friend reads it aloud. Items that the original lecturer put on the board are shown at the top of the lecture. As you take your notes, apply the hints you have learned in this chapter. Then answer the questions that follow the selection by referring to your notes but not to the selection itself. Write your answers on separate sheets of paper.

Lecture about Listening

On Board:

problem of losing attention	spare time
125 WPM = talking speed	three techniques for concentration
500 WPM = listening speed	intend to listen

I'm going to describe to you a listening problem that many people have. I'll also explain why many people have the problem, and I'll tell you what can be done about the problem. The listening problem that many people have is that they lose attention while listening to a speaker. They get bored, their minds wander, their thoughts go elsewhere.

Everyone has had this experience of losing attention, but probably few people understand one of the main reasons why we have this trouble keeping our attention on the speaker. The reason is this: There is a great deal of difference between talking speed and listening speed. The average speaker talks at the rate of 125 words a minute. On the other hand, we can listen and think at the rate of about 500 words a minute. Picture it: The speaker is going along at 125 WPM and we are sitting there ready to move at four times that speed. The speaker is like a tortoise plodding along slowly; we, the listeners, are like the rabbit ready to dash along at a much faster speed. The result of this gap is that we have a lot of spare time to use while listening to a speech.

Unfortunately, many of us use this time to go off on side excursions of our own. We may begin thinking about a date, a sports event, a new shirt we want to buy, balancing our budget, how to start saving money, what we must do later in the day, and a thousand other things. The result of the side excursions may be that, when our attention returns to the speaker, we find that we have been left far behind. The speaker has gotten into some new idea, and we, having missed some connection, have little sense of what is being talked about. We may have to listen very closely for five minutes to get back on track. The temptation at this point is to go back to our own special world of thoughts and forget about the speaker. Then we're wasting both our time and the speaker's time. What we must do, instead, is work hard to keep our attention on the speaker and to concentrate on what is being said.

Here are three mental techniques you can use to keep your concentration on the speaker. First of all, summarize what the speaker has said. Do this after each new point is developed. This constant summarizing will help you pay attention. Second, try to guess where the speaker is going next. Try to anticipate what direction the speaker is going to take, based on what has already been said. This game you play with yourself arouses your curiosity and helps maintain your attention. Third, question the truth, the validity, of the speaker's words. Compare the points made with your own knowledge and experience. Keep trying to decide whether you agree or disagree with the speaker on the basis of what you know. Don't simply take as gospel whatever the speaker tells you; question it—ask yourself whether you think it is true. Remember, then, to summarize what the speaker has said, try to guess where the speaker is going next, and question the truth of what is stated.

All these techniques can make you a better listener. But even better than these three techniques, I think, is that you make a conscious effort to listen more closely. You must intend to concentrate, intend to listen carefully. For example, you should go into your classes every day determined to pay close attention. It should be easier for you to make this important mental decision if you remember how easily attention can wander when someone else is speaking.

Questions on the Lecture:
1. What is a listening problem that many people have?
2. What are common talking and listening speeds?
3. What are three techniques to help you pay attention when someone else is talking?
4. What is the most important step you can take to become a better listener?

6 Follow the directions given for Activity 5.

Lecture about Common Behaviors of a Mass Society

On Board:

common behaviors of a mass society	fad or fashion
rumor	craze
two reasons why rumors spread	mass hysteria

We live in a mass society, and today I'm going to talk about some of the common behaviors that we see in the members of a mass society. The four behaviors that I'll discuss are the rumor, the fad or fashion, the craze, and mass hysteria.

The first type of mass behavior is the rumor. A rumor may be defined as a rapidly spreading report not supported by proven fact. Have you heard that a certain famous brand of bubble gum contains spider eggs? That rumor spread among school children and other people throughout the country for a year or so, even though it had no basis whatsoever in fact. Another equally groundless rumor that spread far and wide was that a famous hamburger chain devoted some of its profits to a church of Satan. And perhaps you heard, several year ago, that Beatle Paul McCartney had died in a mysterious way. McCartney, just like Mark Twain, had to make the public claim, "The reports of my death have been greatly exaggerated."

Rumors can be spread by word of mouth or through the mass media—the nationwide newspapers, magazines, and television and radio networks. You should remember that rumors tend to grow, especially in times of great stress. For example, during the chaos that followed President John Kennedy's assassination, rumors began to circulate that a conspiracy was at work. One rumor was that Lyndon Johnson would be killed next, and then key members of the Cabinet and Congress. Another example of a stress-related rumor is one that was circulated among people living on the East Coast during the Great Blackout in the mid-1960s: the blackout, some said, was caused by a nuclear attack.

Why do people spread rumors? Well, for one thing, people hold onto a rumor if it confirms something they already believe. If you already believed that subversive forces were at work in the country, you would have been quick to feel that those forces were responsible for Kennedy's assassination. In the same way, if you already felt that a worldwide nuclear war was inevitable, you might have interpreted the Great Blackout as a sign of nuclear attack.

The second cause of a rumor is simply people's desire for interesting conversation and gossip. If you hear that two of your coworkers have been called to the boss's office without any apparent reason, a rumor might start that the boss was criticizing their work and was ready to fire them. This is a rumor because there is no evidence that the boss was criticizing them. For all we know, the boss may have been asking them to plan a company picnic. To summarize, then, the two reasons why rumors spread are (1) to support a belief, and (2) to satisfy the desire for gossip.

Let's go on now to the second type of mass behavior—the fad or fashion. A fad may be defined as a trivial, short-lived variation in speech or behavior. It is a mere "flash-in-the-pan" type of event. It flares up quickly and dies. People who want to be the first at doing or buying the latest thing will participate in a fad. "Streaking," or running nude through a public place, was a fad; streakers even appeared at the Olympic games and on the Academy Awards television program when the fad was hot. Another fad was the pet rocks that people bought several years ago as Christmas gifts.

Fashions in clothing are a type of fad. One year it may seem as if everyone is wearing blue jeans with wide bell-bottoms; the next year, all those jeans seem to have turned into the kind with tight, tapered legs. The latest thing in fashion can start at any social level, high or low, and will eventually affect all levels. One interesting point to remember about fashions is that they can be a reflection of the society they appear in. For instance, Victorian clothes were concealing and confining, and were very appropriate in an age obsessed with correctness and the appearance of modesty. In the last several years, the trend has been toward unisex clothing, that is, both sexes wearing basically the same shirts, pants, and jackets. This trend toward unisex clothing reflects our society's attempt to move away from rigidly defined sex roles.

The third type of mass behavior I'm going to talk about is the craze. What is a craze? A craze is a general rush toward some imagined satisfaction. For instance, there can be a craze for gambling in the stock market or for a religious cult. Many times, schemes to make money are crazes; everyone may rush to join a chain letter or to buy land in a place like Arizona or Florida.

Crazes have been around for a long time. Back in the seventeenth century one craze centered around tulip bulbs in Holland. So many people at the time speculated in tulip bulbs that the bulbs became worth their weight in gold. The tulip bulbs were bought, sold, and hoarded like precious stones. Tulip bulbs, and especially rare varieties of tulips, went up in value daily like rising stocks in the market. Of course, a crash eventually came—just as it does for all crazes.

A more recent example of a craze involved LSD. LSD became a craze among a minority of college students, with an estimated 5 or 6 percent having tried LSD at least once when the craze peaked in 1967. With Dr. Timothy Leary as its high priest, LSD was to bring the world into a new land of peace, love, and creativity. But a growing fear of LSD's hazard ended the craze and reduced its users to no more than 1 percent of college students by 1969.

An important point to keep in mind is that the craze differs from ordinary fads in often becoming an obsession for its followers. A fad is always trivial; a craze, as was the case with LSD, can become a very serious matter.

The fourth type of mass behavior is mass hysteria. Mass hysteria may be defined as some form of irrational, compulsive belief or behavior which spreads among people. I'll repeat that. Mass hysteria is some form of irrational, compulsive belief or behavior which spreads among people. For example, some students at a Louisiana high school were once seized by an uncontrollable twitching. First one student began to twitch; then the mysterious twitching spread like wildfire. None of the students was sick or diseased, and there was no physical explanation for the phenomenon. It seemed to be a case of mass hysteria.

Another example of mass hysteria is a rash of flying saucer reports. From an analysis of such reports, it is apparent that early flying saucer reports are often the main reason for later flying saucer reports. People hear about flying saucers in the mass media. Some of these people imagine they see the saucers themselves and call up television stations and newspapers to report new "sightings." It is, of course, a scientific possibility that some of the "unidentified flying objects" are from outer space. However, many scientists feel that the evidence for them is, at the present time, less than convincing.

Let me summarize to this point. We've discussed four kinds of mass behavior: the rumor, the fad or fashion, the craze, and mass hysteria. The question that we must now ask is whether we can explain this collective behavior. All these mass behaviors seem to arise under certain conditions and produce certain results. In general, rumors, fads, crazes, and mass hysteria seem to result from some form of fear, confusion, frustration, or boredom. People use them either to avoid or to try to explain some of the problems of everyday life. It is safe to say that as long as frustration and anxiety exist in our society and in the people of our society, these various forms of mass behavior will continue to appear.

Questions on the Lecture:
1. List four common behaviors of a mass society.
2. Give the definition of a rumor.
3. What are two reasons why people spread rumors?
4. What is an example of a fad?
5. What is a main difference between a craze and a fad?
6. Give the definition of mass hysteria.
7. What is an example of mass hysteria?

7 Follow the directions given for Activity 5.

Lecture about Abraham Maslow's Hierarchy of Needs

On Board:

Maslow's hierarchy of needs	esteem
biological	self-actualization
safety	cognitive
social	aesthetic

Today I'm going to talk about a famous psychological theory, the theory of human needs proposed by Abraham Maslow. The theory is usually referred to as Maslow's hierarchy of needs. Early in his professional life, Maslow began to study human motivation, or what causes people to act the way they do. He decided that people have certain needs and that all human behavior is an attempt to satisfy these needs. Maslow listed human needs in a particular order, from the most basic to the highest needs. A ranking of items like this is called a *hierarchy*; this is why Maslow called his theory a hierarchy of needs. Maslow believed that the higher needs in the hierarchy do not significantly influence people's behavior until their most basic needs are satisfied. Maslow listed seven human needs, from most basic to highest. I will discuss each need individually.

The most basic human needs, and the first item in Maslow's hierarchy, are the *biological needs.* Biological needs are those needed to survive. Humans need food, water, and air to survive as individuals. These needs must be satisfied before people can think of anything else. For example, if you are starving, all your energy will be directed toward finding food. You will not be worried about making new friends, or getting an "A" on an exam, or being liked—all higher needs on the hierarchy.

Hunger is the biological need that has been studied most extensively. Maslow's theory says that if the need for food is not satisfied, it will become more important than any other need. An experiment conducted during World War II proved this. A group of young men were given a diet which provided them with half the number of calories they normally consumed. These men were then housed in a dormitory for twenty-four weeks. Because their need for food was not satisfied, they became obsessed with the idea of food. They dreamed about food; they read cookbooks; they replaced their girlfriends' pictures with pictures of steaks. They argued with each other over tidbits of food. They could not joke, express friendly feelings, or keep their minds on their work. The biological need for food overshadowed all other needs.

Humans have other biological needs beside food, water, and air. For example, human beings have sex drives which they try to satisfy. Although sexual activity is not essential for the indvidual to survive, it is necessary for the species to survive. If humans stopped reproducing themselves, there wouldn't be a human race anymore. To sum up, then, biological needs must be met to maintain individual life and to preserve the human species.

After biological needs have been met, people's behavior will be directed toward satisfying *safety needs.* Safety needs are the second item in Maslow's hierarchy. Safety needs may be defined as security and freedom from danger. Every human being needs to feel protected from harm. The family is an important institution to fulfill safety needs because it protects helpless infants and young children. Our needs for safety are shown not just in the institution of the family. You can see our need for safety in the fact that, as adults, we want jobs with security; we save money for emergencies; and we purchase insurance policies. All these represent our attempts to protect ourselves from harm. Our need for safety may also be shown in our preference for familiar rather than unfamiliar things. Many people, for example, know and trust franchised businesses like McDonald's or Howard Johnson's. Therefore, when they travel to unfamiliar areas of the country, they may eat and sleep only in familiar, known surroundings. They know what to expect and feel safe in such surroundings. Many elderly people, especially, tend to fear the new and the unfamiliar. Perhaps this is one reason why older people become "set in their ways" and distrust any sudden change.

After their biological and safety needs are met, people will try to fulfill their *social needs.* These social needs, the third item in Maslow's hierarchy, can be defined as the need to belong to a group and to give and receive love. If human beings' biological and safety needs are consistently fulfilled, they will seek out the companionship and love of other people. All of us need friends and close companions. We have a strong desire to associate with others, to join groups, clubs, and organizations. As children, we enjoy family life and create families when we mature.

Not surprisingly, people feel unhappy when they are not accepted socially. Belonging to a group gives people friends in time of trouble and companions to laugh and have fun with. Belonging to a group makes people feel needed and wanted. You should remember that wanting to marry is partially an attempt to satisfy the need to belong. A mate provides warmth, affection, shared pleasure, companionship, and security. For these reasons, as well as for satisfaction of the sex drive, most human beings seek out lifelong partners. Our need for love and belonging is so powerful, in fact, that emotional scars result when children are unwanted and rejected. Unloved children may become mentally unstable or hostile adults. They may grow up to be cold and uncaring and, in some cases, may even adopt criminal behavior. That is why Maslow rates the social need to belong and feel loved directly after the most basic needs for physical survival and safety.

Esteem needs are the fourth item in Maslow's hierarchy. By esteem needs, Maslow means that all people need to respect themselves and to feel that others respect them. Self-esteem means caring about yourself, feeling that you are a unique and valuable person. How, you may ask, do people develop these positive feelings about themselves? The important answer is that they develop positive feelings by achieving personally meaningful goals. The goals may be related to family life, school, work, or community service. For example, a person may decide to earn a college degree, to aim for a promotion at work, to become a better parent. Achieving any of these goals is a rewarding feeling. Any external benefits, like an increase in salary or wider job opportunities, take second place to the internal satisfaction associated with goal achievement. Achievement, in turn, raises a person's self-esteem or sense of individual worth. People who achieve goals not only enhance their own self-esteem but also earn the respect of others.

It should be noted, however, that as a person's self-esteem is strengthened, the need for the esteem of others is diminished. Individuals who lack confidence often spend a lot of energy doing things that they hope will gain other people's approval. On the other hand, people who are self-confident work, not for the praise of others, but for the internal satisfaction that comes with goal achievement. For them, it is more important to measure up to their own than to somebody else's standards.

If people are lucky enough to have their biological, safety, social, and esteem needs fulfilled, what other needs could possibly exist? Needs five, six, and seven in Maslow's hierarchy are called the "higher" needs. Many of us never try to satisfy these needs because we are too preoccupied with satisfying the first four needs. Remember, people can move on to a higher need only if their more basic needs are fulfilled.

To be more specific, the fifth item in Maslow's hierarchy is the *self-actualization need*. This is defined as the need to become what one is capable of becoming or, in other words, to live up to one's potential. Self-actualization, to repeat, is the need to live up to one's potential. After basis needs have been satisfied, people are liable to feel discontented and restless unless they do what is important to them and what they feel they are suited for. For example, to feel self-actualized, athletes must participate in sports, musicians must make music, students must commit themselves to their studies. The need to self-actualize never ends because people continually set new levels of achievement for themselves. Striving to reach personally meaningful goals is a gratifying process. For example, people who play a sport will usually do the best they can. Knowing they are striving to work at their best level satisfies their need to self-actualize.

Sometimes, of course, it is impossible to self-actualize. People may be prevented from achieving their full potential. For instance, children with musical talent who have no money to purchase lessons or instruments will probably not reach their potential and will probably feel somewhat disappointed and frustrated.

Next in Maslow's hierarchy, the sixth kind of needs, are the *cognitive needs*. These are the needs to know and understand. All children are curious. They want to know how things work. They ask questions; they take things apart. Curiosity, it is important to remember, is an expression of the human need to know and understand the world. Often, however, children's natural curiosity is lost by the time they reach adulthood. Although there are several reasons why this happens, many experts think that school is the primary cause. Some children have bad experiences in school; they may, for example, be discouraged from questioning or they may be given a lot of busy work to do. In these situations, children may come to associate learning with drudgery and lose the joy of learning. Adults' curiosity may also be suppressed unless they feel extremely safe and secure. I mentioned earlier today that some adults are frightened by the new and the unfamiliar. Curious people plunge into unknown and unfamiliar territory. To be able to live with and even look forward to uncertainty, people's safety needs must first be met.

Satisfying the need to know and understand leads to a fuller, more enjoyable life. People who are constantly learning new things take more interest in life. The famous author E. B. White once said that the joy of learning about new things is the one experience that survives the inevitable tragedies of life. Those people who find a joy in learning are never bored. They become interested in new hobbies and fields of study. They read books, magazines, and newspapers to satisfy their desire to know. Discovering the new and the unknown can even become a career. Scientists and researchers, for example, constantly strive to widen the boundaries of their knowledge.

I'll now talk about the final item in Maslow's hierarchy, the *aesthetic needs*. These may be defined as an appreciation of the beautiful. Human beings satisfy their aesthetic needs by taking pleasure in beautiful things—the pleasing patterns of sounds, shapes, colors, and words. More specifically, they take pleasure in paintings, sculpture, nature, plays, novels, poetry, architecture, photographs, other people. Children, of course, openly express their enjoyment of "pretty things." Some adults, however, seem to lose this ability to enjoy the beauty in the world. Males, especially, are often uncomfortable acknowledging their aesthetic needs. That is unfortunate because there is great satisfaction in remaining open to the pleasure that comes with enjoying beautiful things.

To sum up, I have discussed Maslow's hierarchy of needs. According to Maslow, basic needs must be satisfied before the higher needs can influence behavior. We must remember, however, that this is only one theory of what motivates human behavior. There are other theories as well that increase our understanding of why we act as we do. We should also keep in mind that human beings rarely respond to only one need at a time. Buying a new house, for instance, may be the result of a mixture of needs—the need for safety, the need for the esteem of others, even the need for belonging and love. Needs may also come into conflict with each other. For example, when parents risk their lives to save their children, they are placing love needs over safety needs. In short, the way our needs influence our behavior is not always clear-cut. Still, Maslow's theory is invaluable. It can help us understand more about the complexities of human behavior. And increased understanding is sure to have some effect on how we conduct our lives and how we deal with other people.

Questions on the Lecture:
1. List in order of importance Maslow's hierarchy of needs.
2. Name three biological needs that all humans have.
3. What is one way that people show their need for safety?
4. Define social needs.
5. How do people develop positive feelings about themselves?
6. Define the self-actualization need.
7. Curiosity is an expression of which of the higher needs?
8. How may aesthetic needs be defined?

8 Read the following description of one student's study situation:

Howard has trouble taking notes in all his classes. He is seldom sure about what is important enough to write down. Also, he has trouble organizing material in any way when he does write it down. Often the only points he records are the ones the teacher puts on the board. The connections between these points are usually clear to him in class, for he spends most of his time listening carefully to the teacher rather than taking notes. However, several weeks later when he is studying for a test, he has trouble remembering many of the relationships among points. His notes do not provide a complete, unified picture of the subject but seem to consist of many isolated bits of information.

One course that gives Howard special problems is Sociology. In class the teacher asks students questions and uses their comments as takeoff points for discussing key ideas. Sometimes she may be five minutes into a key idea before Howard realizes it is important—and he hasn't even begun to take notes. He often winds up with such a frustrating shortage of notes that he decides not to go to class at all. In another course, Biology, the teacher talks so fast that Howard cannot keep up. Also, he misspells so many words that it is often impossible for him to understand his notes when he tries to read them over weeks later before an exam.

Now write a one-page (or longer) essay in which you answer *in detail* the question, "What can Howard do to become a better notetaker?" In your answer, apply the information you have learned in this chapter on taking and studying class notes.

4

Reading and Studying Textbooks I:

Two Study Systems

This chapter will show you how to:

- Preview a textbook selection
- Read and mark the selection
- Write study notes on the selection
- Recite the study notes until you remember them

If you have trouble reading and studying your textbooks, you may think, as do many students, that the solution is to sign up for a speed-reading course. Chances are, however, that you don't need to increase your reading speed as much as you need to develop a sound overall approach to reading and studying assigned material.

This chapter describes two general approaches for you to use when reading and studying textbook selections: the SQ3R system and the PRWR system. The second approach, which has several features in common with the first, will be discussed in detail. You should choose the approach or combination of approaches that seems most comfortable and effective for your particular study needs.

THE SQ3R STUDY SYSTEM

The SQ3R system is taught by many reading teachers. The letters stand for the five steps in the process: (1) Survey, (2) Question, (3) Read, (4) Recite, (5) Review. Explanations of the five steps follow.

1 Survey, or preview, the article or textbook chapter, using the process described on pages 46 and 47.

2 Convert the first heading in the selection into a question or a series of questions. (You may want to write the questions above the heading or on a separate piece of paper.) For example, if the heading is "The Myth of the Southern Gentleman," you might ask the questions: "What was the myth of the Southern Gentleman?" and "Why was it a myth?" It's a good idea to jot down your answers in the margin of your textbook or on a sheet of paper. (You will be given some practice turning headings into basic questions on page 76.)

3 Read the section to find the answers to the questions. Also, try to identify other important points in the material by forming additional questions such as: What is the main idea in the paragraph? What is the supporting material for the idea? How does this paragraph relate to preceding points? Then read to find the answers to the questions. Asking questions and then reading to find the answers will help you concentrate on the material; your mind will be less apt to wander.

4   Immediately after completing a section, look away and see if you can recite to yourself the answers to your questions. This recitation helps you see exactly what you do and don't know. (You may want to write your answers down on a separate sheet. If you do, keep your notes brief and try to use your own words rather than those in the book.) Go on then to repeat steps 2, 3, and 4 in the remaining sections of the material.

5   After you complete all the sections, review the entire selection. See whether you can recite the answers to all the questions you formed.

THE PRWR STUDY SYSTEM

The PRWR system has much in common with the approach just described. The letters here stand for the four steps in the process: (1) Preview, (2) Read, (3) Write, (4) Recite. Here is a summary of the four steps:

1   Preview the selection.

2   Read and mark the selection. Pay special attention to definitions, enumerations, headings and subheadings (the last two may be turned into questions), signal words, and main ideas in paragraphs. (See pages 65 to 72 for full explanations of these items.)

3   Write study notes on the selection.

4   Recite the study notes until you remember them.

These steps are explained in detail in the pages ahead.

STEP 1   PREVIEW THE SELECTION

Previewing is the first step in reading an article or textbook chapter. A preview is a five- or six-minute survey that provides you with a bird's-eye view of what you are reading. The preview can often give you a good initial sense of the main topics and ideas in the material and can help you understand the general organization of a selection. Here is how to preview a selection:

1 **Study the title.** The title gives you in a few words the shortest possible summary of the whole selection. Without reading a line of the text, you can learn in a general way what the material is about. For example, if the first chapter of a sociology book is titled "Science and Search for Truth," you can expect a general discussion about the methods and goals of science rather than a specific treatment of, say, social institutions or the structure of the family.

2 **Read over quickly the first and last several paragraphs of the material.** These paragraphs may describe briefly the main ideas in the selection.

3 **Look quickly for relationships among the various headings and subheadings.** Are there many main headings? Each one probably deals with an important aspect of the topic in the chapter. Do the subheads under a main head relate to it in any obvious way? Relationships between main and subheads are often keys to important ideas in a chapter.

   Most texts use two or three orders of headings. Main headings are usually in larger typeface; they also may be set off by capital letters or different-colored ink. Subheadings are usually in smaller type; they may be underlined, capitalized, italicized, or set in from the margin. For example, note the main heads and subheads in the textbook selection that follows. Sub-subheadings are often set off under the subheadings and are in smaller letters.

4 **Dip into the text here or there.** At random, read the first sentences of some paragraphs. Note the words the author has emphasized by setting them off in *italic* type; try to spot definitions and basic enumerations (see pages 65 to 67). Finally, look briefly at pictures, diagrams, and graphs; all are often used to illustrate main ideas.

   Many students are understandably reluctant to spend a little time getting an overall picture of assigned material. They were never taught to preview and so are not aware of the value of this technique. If you are conditioned by past experience not to survey a selection, you may have to work at breaking a mental set and simply force yourself to preview. The effort, however, will be well worth it.

   • Preview the textbook selection on the next page.
   • Activities for previewing a textbook chapter and a full textbook are on pages 57 and 58.

A TEXTBOOK SELECTION

ALTERNATIVES TO CONFLICT

The conflict process may operate at so great a cost that people often seek to avoid it. Conflict is often avoided through some form of three other processes: *accommodation, assimilation,* and *amalgamation.*

Accommodation

> *It threw me when my folks got a divorce right after I graduated. I guess I took them for granted. Our home always seemed to me about like most others. At graduation, Dad took me aside and said that he and Mom were calling it quits. He said that they had bugged each other for years but now that I would be on my own, they were going to separate.*

The above story, adapted from a student's life history, is an example of accommodation, a process of developing temporary working agreements between conflicting individuals or groups. It develops when persons or groups find it necessary to work together despite their hostilities and differences. In accommodation, no real settlement of issues is reached; each group retains its own goals and viewpoints, but arrives at an "agreement to disagree" without fighting. Some of the different forms of accommodation are described below.

DISPLACEMENT   Displacement is the process of suspending one conflict by replacing it with another. A classic example is the threat of war to end internal conflicts and bring national unity.

Finding a scapegoat is a favorite displacement technique. The term refers to an ancient Hebrew ceremony in which the sins of the people were symbolically heaped upon a goat which was driven into the wilderness. Unpopular minorities often become scapegoats. For example, in newly independent countries, all the problems of the new nation may be blamed upon the remaining "colonial influences."

INSTITUTIONALIZED RELEASE OF HOSTILITY   In many societies, there are some institutionalized provisions for release of hostilities and tensions. Some primitive tribes regulated combat in a manner designed to express aggression, yet avoid destructive warfare. In our society, spectator sports, especially contact sports like football, hockey, boxing, and wrestling, may be examples of an institutionalized release of hostility. They can all be seen as easing the pressure toward conflict.

TOLERATION   In some conflicts, victory is impossible and compromise undesirable. Toleration is an agreement to disagree peaceably. Religious conflict is a classic example of this situation. In Europe at the time of the Reformation, both Protestants and Catholics were positive that they had the "true" version of the Christian faith. Neither group was willing to compromise, and in spite of severe conflict, neither group could destroy the other. Adjustment was made on the basis of toleration; each church ceased to persecute other churches while continuing to hold that these other churches were in error.

Assimilation

Whenever groups meet, some mutual interchange or diffusion of culture takes place. This two-way process by which persons and groups come to share a common culture is called assimilation. Assimilation reduces group conflicts by blending different groups into larger, culturally homogenous groups. The bitter riots against the Irish and the discriminations against the Scandinavians in the United States disappeared as assimilation erased the group differences and blurred the sense of separate group identity.

Amalgamation

Amalgamation is the biological interbreeding of two groups until they become one. For instance, wholesale amalgamation ended the conflicts of the Anglo-Saxons with the Norman invaders of England. An incomplete amalgamation, however, generally creates a status- and conflict-filled system where status is measured by blood "purity" as in Central America and parts of South America.

STEP 2   READ AND MARK THE SELECTION

Read the material completely for all you can understand the first time around. Do not allow yourself to get stalled by what you don't understand.

Perhaps you are wondering why you should read through without stopping the first time. If you stop to puzzle over points you don't understand, you may never finish even a first reading of a selection. But what you *do* understand from previewing and then reading the material once will help you when you go back later to spots where you at first had some difficulty.

As you read, look for and mark off what seem to be important ideas and details. The markings you make in this first reading will help you proceed much more confidently when you do a closer and more selective reading. At that time, you will not have to read everything again, because the preview and the first reading will have given you a sense of how the material is organized, where the important points are, and what areas you must reread so you can take clear, effective study notes.

Marking means that you underline, check, star, number or otherwise signal important points in a selection. The purpose of marking is to set off certain points so that you can easily return to them later when you take study notes.

Marking should be an active process, reflecting your decisions about what is significant in the material you're reading. (When you previewed, you noted some key ideas, examples, definitions, and enumerations. The work you did then will make marking easier now.)

Marking should also be a selective process. Some students are so impressed by all the markings they enter in their textbooks that they delude themselves into thinking they've done the hard work needed to pull the material together. However, setting off too much material is no better than setting off too little. In short, mark off something only when you are fairly sure it is significant. Usually, you will have to read to the end of a paragraph or section before you know whether something is important. Then go back and mark.

What to Mark

Students often ask, "How can I tell what is important enough to mark, especially on the first reading?" All the following are keys to important material in the selection you are studying:

1. Definitions and examples
2. Enumerations (items in a list)
3. Headings and subheadings and relationships between them
4. Signal words
5. Main ideas in paragraphs and short selections

Each of these will be discussed in detail in the next chapter.

How to Mark

Here are some hints about how to mark important ideas.

1 Set off definitions by underlining them and writing *Def* in the margin.

2 Set off helpful examples by writing *Ex* in the margin. Do not underline examples.

3 Use numbers (1, 2, 3, etc.) to mark enumerations (items in a list).

4 Underline ideas of obvious importance. You might also set off important ideas by putting *Imp* or an asterisk (*) in the margin.

    Put a vertical line in the margin to set off important material that is several lines in length. Do not underline these longer sections because the page will end up being so cluttered that you'll find it difficult to make any sense of the markings.

    Use a check (√) to mark off items that *may* be important.

- Read and mark the textbook selection you already previewed on pages 48 and 49.

STEP 3   WRITE STUDY NOTES ON THE SELECTION

After you have previewed and then read and marked a textbook selection, you are ready to study the material. There are two methods you may use. You can either write notes in the margin of the text itself, or you can prepare separate sheets of study notes. The first method is quicker, but the second method is more thorough. Each method is explained on the pages that follow.

First Method: Jot Recall Words in the Textbook Margin

After using the first two steps to locate important material, reread the selection. Then write down key words in the margin of the text to help you recall the important information.

Look at the marked textbook selection that starts below. Note in the margin the series of recall words that can be used to pull into memory the key concepts in the selection.

Once key or recall words have been jotted in the margin, they can be used to study the material on each page. Simply convert each key word into a question and review the material until you can recite the answer without looking at the page. For example, the recall words in the selection could be turned into such questions as: "What are three alternatives to conflict?" "What is the definition of accommodation?" "What is an example of accommodation?" "What are the three forms of accommodation?"

A TEXTBOOK SELECTION

ALTERNATIVES TO CONFLICT

3 alternatives to conflict   The conflict process may operate at so great a cost that people often seek to avoid it. Conflict is often avoided through some form of three other processes: *accommodation, assimilation,* and *amalgamation.*

1 **Accommodation**

Ex of accommodation   *It threw me when my folks got a divorce right after I graduated. I guess I took them for granted. Our home always seemed to me about like most others. At graduation, Dad took me aside and said that he and Mom were calling it quits. He said that they had bugged each other for years but now that I would be on my own, they were going to separate.*

Def of accommodation   The above story, adapted from a student's life history, is an example of accommodation, <u>a process of developing temporary working agreements between conflicting individuals or groups</u>. It develops when persons or groups find it necessary to work together despite their hostilities and differences. In accommodation, no real settlement of issues is reached; each group retains its own goals and viewpoints, but arrives at an "agreement to disagree" without fighting. Some of the different forms of accommodation are

3 forms of accommodation   described below.

a DISPLACEMENT   Displacement is the process of suspending one conflict by replacing it with another. A classic example is the threat of war to end internal conflicts and bring national unity.

Def + ex of displacement

Finding a scapegoat is a favorite displacement technique. The term refers to an ancient Hebrew ceremony in which the sins of the people were symbolically heaped upon a goat which was driven into the wilderness. Unpopular minorities often become scapegoats. For example, in newly independent countries, all the problems of the new nation may be blamed upon the remaining "colonial influences."

Favorite displacement technique +ex

b INSTITUTIONALIZED RELEASE OF HOSTILITY   In many societies, there are some institutionalized provisions for release of hostilities and tensions. Some primitive tribes regulated combat in a manner designed to express aggression, yet avoid destructive warfare. In our society, spectator sports, especially contact sports like football, hockey, boxing, and wrestling may be examples of an instititutionalized release of hostility. They can all be seen as easing the pressure toward conflict.

Ex of inst. release

c TOLERATION   In some conflicts, victory is impossible and compromise undesirable. Toleration is an agreement to disagree peaceably. Religious conflict is a classic example of this situation. In Europe at the time of the Reformation, both Protestants and Catholics were positive that they had the "true" version of the Christian faith. Neither group was willing to compromise, and in spite of severe conflict, neither group could destroy the other. Adjustment was made on the basis of toleration; each church ceased to persecute other churches while continuing to hold that these other churches were in error.

Def + ex of toleration

2 Assimilation

Whenever groups meet, some mutual interchange or diffusion of culture takes place. This two-way process by which persons and groups come to share a common culture is called assimilation. Assimilation reduces group conflicts by blending different groups into larger, culturally homogenous groups. The bitter riots against the Irish and the discriminations against the Scandinavians in the United States disappeared as assimilation erased the group differences and blurred the sense of separate group identity.

Def + ex of assimilation

3 Amalgamation

Amalgamation is the biological interbreeding of two groups until they become one. For instance, wholesale amalgamation ended the conflicts of the Anglo-Saxons with the Norman invaders of England. An incomplete amalgamation, however, generally creates a status- and conflict-filled system where status is measured by blood "purity" as in Central America and parts of South America.

Def + ex of amalgamation

Second Method: Prepare Separate Sheets of Study Notes

After using the first two steps to locate important material, reread the selection. Then prepare separate sheets of study notes on the important information. On page 55 are sample study notes for the textbook selection on "Alternatives to Conflict."

Writing study notes has two major advantages. First, taking notes forces you to concentrate; you must decide what is important and so should be written down. Second, having the material in study note form gives you a psychological boost; you have reduced many textbook pages to a relatively small amount of material to be studied.

Because you have done so much preliminary work, notetaking on separate sheets should not be so difficult. Keep the following points in mind as you take notes:

1 Give the name of the textbook, the author(s), and the chapter title at the top of the first sheet of your study notes.

2 Make your handwriting clear and easy to read. Before a test, you want to direct your energy to studying your notes, not trying to decipher them.

3 Don't just copy, word for word, parts of the original material into your notes. As much as possible, record the information in your own words. That will help you understand the selection more easily.

4 Do not overuse outlining symbols and create an unnecessarily complicated outline. You do *not* need to put a symbol in front of each item in your notes. Often a simple sequence of numbers (1, 2, 3, etc.) and letters (*a, b, c,* etc.), indented words, and abbreviations (*Def, Ex,* and so on) will be enough to signal relationships among parts of the material. Note, for example, how few outlining symbols are used on the study sheet on page 55, yet how clear the organization is.

If you find that you do occasionally need additional symbols to take notes, use the following sequence:

Roman numerals: I, II, III, etc.
  Capital letters: A, B, C, etc.
    Numbers: 1, 2, 3, etc.
      Small letters: a, b, c, etc.
        Numbers in parentheses: (1) (2), (3), etc.
          Small letters in parentheses: (a), (b), (c), etc.

You will note that main headings are at the margin. The next level is indented about half an inch from the margin. Third- and fourth-level headings are indented even further.

5   Remember to number enumerations (items in a series). Thus in the study notes on page 55, the three alternatives to conflict are numbered 1, 2, and 3. Enumerations are often signaled in the original material by such words as *first, second, next, another, in addition, moreover, also,* and *finally.* At other times, enumerations are apparent in the relationships between headings and subheadings. For example, in the textbook selection on page 48, the three alternatives to conflict (*Accommodation, Assimilation,* and *Amalgamation*) are presented as three subheads that follow the main head. Similarly, there are three sub-subheads (*Displacement, Institutionalized release of hostility,* and *Toleration*) that fit under *Accommodation.* Enumerations help authors organize their material and will help you take notes on that material.

Always begin a series of main points at the same spot on the margin. By so doing, you make visually clear the relationship among the major parts of the material. Similarly, always indent a series of subpoints under main points, and keep the subpoints at the same spot of indentation. Thus in the study notes on page 55, subpoints *a, b,* and *c* under "Three forms of accommodation" appear at the same spot of indentation.

Finally, be sure to include a heading for each list of items. For instance, the heading for the major enumeration in the study notes on page 55 was "Three Alternatives to Conflict." And there was a heading, "Three forms of accommodation," for the secondary enumeration.

6   Follow, as a general rule, the author's order of headings when you take notes on an entire chapter. Put the main order of headings at the margin. Indent (set in about half an inch from the margin) the next order of headings. Indent even further a third and possibly a fourth order of headings.

7   Summarize material whenever possible; that is, reduce it to the fewest possible words while still keeping the idea complete and clear. In the sample study notes on page 55, the example of accommodation has been summarized so that it reads simply, "Parents agree to wait until child graduates to separate."

Summarizing is explained in detail on pages 135 to 138.

8   Be sure to go through the study notes you have prepared on separate sheets and, in the margin, jot down key words to help you recall the main ideas you identified.

Sociology, Horton and Hunt, Chapter 14: "Social Processes"

Three Alternatives to Conflict
1. Accommodation — a process of developing temporary working agreements between conflicting individuals or groups.
   Ex. — Parents agree to wait until child graduates to separate.

   Three forms of accommodation:
   a. Displacement — process of suspending one conflict by replacing it with another.
      Ex. — Threat of war to bring national unity
      Favorite displacement technique: find a scapegoat.
      Ex. — blame problems of new nation on "colonial influences."
   b. Institutionalized release of hostility
      Ex — specator sports used in our society to ease pressure toward conflict
   c. Toleration — agreement to disagree peaceably.
      Ex. — Protestants and Catholics during Reformation came to tolerate rather than persecute each other.

2. Assimilation — two-way process by which persons and groups come to share a common culture.
      Ex — riots against Irish in the US ceased as they were assimilated.

3. Amalgamation — biological interbreeding of two groups until they become one.
      Ex — Anglo-Saxon and Norman invaders of England became one, ending conflicts.

STEP 4   RECITE THE STUDY NOTES
UNTIL YOU REMEMBER THEM

After you have previewed, read, marked, and taken notes on a chapter, you want to ensure that you remember the material. To do this, divide information into sections. Use the recall words written in the margin of your textbook or study sheet to test yourself on the key ideas in each section.

Convert the recall words into questions and review the material until you can recite the answer without looking at the page. For example, the first recall words jotted in the textbook and study sheet margins are "3 alternatives to conflict." Turn those into the question "What are three alternatives to conflict?" and recite the answer without referring to the text or your study notes. When you can recite the answer without looking at the page, go on to the next recall word, convert it into a question, and recite the answer until you can say it without looking at your textbook or your notes. After mastering the idea associated with each new recall word, always go back and retest yourself to make sure you remember the ideas connected to the previous recall words.

This *repeated* self-testing is the key to effective memorization. Your aim is to reach a point where you can recite all your notes without looking at them. When you reach this point, you are not likely to block or panic on exams. (The process of repeated self-testing is described in detail on pages 85 to 88.)

You should prepare and recite your study notes on a regular basis during the semester. When you do, you will be taking advantage of the fact that a series of short study sessions is more effective than a single long session. Also, to offset the forgetting that occurs constantly, you should devote part of each study session to a review of previous material. If you study and review consistently, you will not have to cram the last days before an exam. Instead, you can devote that time to a final intensive review of all the material in the course.

- *Note:* If you have the time, you may find it helpful to *write out* the material you are testing yourself on. The act of writing may fix the material more solidly in your mind than if you simply recited it to yourself.

Activities

1 Review the chapter carefully. Then, without looking back, answer the following questions.

  1. Circle the one thing you should not do when previewing a selection:
     a. Study the title.
     b. Read over the first and last paragraphs.
     c. Write down important ideas.
     d. Look for relationships between headings and subheadings.

  2. Use _____ to mark off each point in an enumeration (a list of items).

  3. True or false: _____ Sometimes you will have to read to the end of a paragraph or section before you will know whether something is important enough to mark off.

  4. Which of the following are values of notetaking?
     a. It forces you to make decisions about what is important enough to write down.
     b. It helps you increase your understanding of the material.
     c. It is a first step toward remembering the material.
     d. All of the above.

  5. When writing study notes on a chapter, you should leave space in the margin for:
     a. Definitions   c. Headings
     b. Enumerations   d. Recall words

2 Previewing a chapter On separate paper, answer the following questions by previewing a chapter in one of your textbooks.

  1. What is the whole chapter about? (This question can usually be answered by giving the title of the chapter.)

  2. How many main headings are there in the chapter?

  3. How many subheads are there in the chapter?

  4. Do any of the subheads relate, in an obvious way, to the main head under which they are found? If so, give an example.

  5. Does the opening (or first few) paragraph(s) give a survey of the chapter?

6. Does the closing (or last few) paragraph(s) give a summary of the chapter?

7. How many charts, diagrams, pictures, tables, or graphs are included in the chapter?

8. How many times is *italic* or **boldface** type used in the chapter?

9. List three terms that appear in italic or boldface type in the chapter.

3 Previewing an entire textbook Previewing an entire textbook can help you use it more efficiently. The preview can give you a quick, general sense of the book's purpose and organization. To preview a textbook, do the following:

1. Look at the opening pages to check the publishing date. (If several dates are given, look for the latest one.) This information will tell you whether the book provides recent material on a subject.

2. Read the preface to get an idea of the author's purpose in writing the book. The author may also describe briefly the organization of the book.

3. Go through the table of contents to get some sense of how the book is organized. (Also, referring to the table of contents during the semester may help you see the relationship among various topics covered in the course.)

4. Finally, flip through the pages of the book at random. Note the kinds of headings and subheadings that are used. See if there are introductions to and summaries of each chapter as well as study questions at the ends of chapters. Look quickly at charts, diagrams, and pictures. Check the end of the book for a glossary (definitions of terms used in the book), an index (page references for information presented in the book), a bibliography (list of information sources cited in the book), and an appendix (supplementary material).

   Use one of your books to complete the textbook preview that follows.

• Name of textbook (include subtitle, if any): _____

_____

• Author: _____

- Date of publication (choose the most recent date if several are listed): _____
- Does the preface explain how the book is organized?_____
  If so, what is one way the book is organized? _____
  _____
- Does the preface talk about the author's purpose in writing the book? _____ If so, what is the purpose? _____
  _____
  _____
- What is one other point made in the preface? _____
  _____
  _____
- How many chapters are in the book? _____
- What is the title of the first chapter? _____
- Are several chapters ever grouped into units or parts?_____
- If so, how many parts are there in the book? _____
- Does the book use:
  a. Italicized words? _____
  b. Boldface print? _____
  c. Several kinds of headings in each chapter? _____
  d. Summaries? _____
  e. Questions at the ends of chapters? _____
  f. Other study aids at the ends of chapters? _____
  g. Photographs? _____
  h. Charts, graphs, tables? _____
- At the end of the book is there:
  a. A glossary? _____
  b. An index? _____
  c. An appendix? _____
  d. A bibliography? _____

4   Reading and marking a textbook selection   Preview and then read and mark the selection below on "The Importance of Attention." Remember to be selective. Mark only the most important points: definitions, key examples, enumerations, main ideas in paragraphs, and son on. (You might want to review the material on page 50.)

THE IMPORTANCE OF ATTENTION

All of us know from personal experience that attention and learning are closely related. When we pay attention—eagerly and single-mindedly—

learning tends to be easy. When we do not pay attention, learning tends to be difficult or even impossible. But, as every student knows, these simple facts are not in themselves very helpful. Try as we may to pay attention, we often fail. While listening to a classroom lecture, we may find ourselves giving our attention not to the words but to the sound of rain on the windowpanes. Reading a textbook, we may find ourselves thinking how pleasant it would be to have a hamburger or go to sleep.

Why is attention so important? And what are the factors that sometimes help us pay attention and sometimes turn our thoughts elsewhere? What, if anything, can we do to control these factors? . . .

Motivation and Attention

One powerful aid to paying attention is motivation. Some people seem to have an almost insatiable thirst for knowledge—any kind of knowledge. They find it easy to pay attention regardless of the subject matter. Some students who are motivated mostly by the desire for good grades also pay close attention regardless of whether they are studying psychology, philosophy, or ancient history. Most of us, however, are somewhat more selective. We are most likely to pay attention when we are learning something that seems to satisfy our own particular and rather specialized motives.

If we can somehow relate the subject matter to our motives, attention can usually be sharpened. Thus the study of Spanish becomes easier if students keep reminding themselves that they may someday be traveling or even working in a Spanish-speaking country.

Feedback and Attention

Psychologists have long been aware that *feedback*, a term borrowed from the field of automation, plays an important role in learning. Feedback means information on how well the learning process is going—that is, on how we are progressing, how much we have learned, how many mistakes we are making and what kinds of mistakes.

One reason feedback helps is that it enables us to correct our mistakes. For example, if we try to learn typing on a dummy keyboard, we may keep hitting the wrong keys without ever knowing it. On an actual typewriter, feedback from the printed page tells us at once when we make a mistake.

Another reason—even more important—is that feedback helps capture and hold attention. By providing evidence that learning is actually taking place, it maintains our interest. If we are strongly motivated to learn, it shows us that we are beginning to satisfy our motives and thus encourages us to go on.

One of the most interesting applications of feedback has been the development of programmed learning, in which the content of a course is broken down into a series of very small steps. At each step a single new term or new idea is introduced or material that has been covered previously is reviewed. When programmed learning is offered in printed form, . . . students ordinarily fill in a blank or several blanks at each step. They can then uncover the correct answer—and get immediate feedback as to whether their response was right or wrong—before going on to the next step. . . .

Rewards

At times, and under certain conditions, rewards may sharpen our attention and spur us on to do the work required in learning. Psychologists speak of two kinds of rewards, each worthy of separate discussion.

1. *External Rewards*

   Some rewards, known as external rewards (or extrinsic rewards), come from the outside. Babies are rewarded for each new accomplishment with a smile and a pat. Older children are rewarded with gold stars, candy, and trips to the movies. Even college students are rewarded for learning—with good grades and eventually diplomas, and sometimes with increased allowances or presents from their parents. All these tokens of success are in a sense merely bribes provided by another person. Nonetheless, they can be effective and useful.

   In one study that demonstrated the value of external rewards, a psychologist worked for a period of years with about 400 boys between the ages of thirteen and eighteen who had done so badly in school that they were considered "uneducable." To give them an incentive to learn, he first paid them small sums of money, then later rewarded them for successes by permitting them to study subjects that they especially liked. On the average these boys managed to cover between two and three years of schoolwork in a single year, and even their scores on intelligence tests improved substantially. The psychologist has concluded that the external rewards of money and permission to study favored subjects served to get the boys going—and finally to reach the point where they really began to enjoy learning.

2. *Internal Rewards*

   The second group of rewards is internal rewards, also sometimes called intrinsic rewards. These are inward feelings of personal satisfaction. They might be called the pleasure of learning for the sake of learning.

   An example is children learning to ride their first bicycle. In part their attention may be drawn by external rewards, such as the respect of their friends. But the rewards are primarily internal— pleasant feelings arising from the satisfaction of their desire to prove their ability and from the sense of power derived from traveling faster on wheels than they can travel on foot. Other examples are adults who try very hard to learn to dance, to play a musical instrument, or to take beautiful photographs. Their attention is absolutely riveted on the learning situation—not because they seek any external reward but because they want the internal reward of learning a new skill, the reward that comes from meeting an internal standard of perfection. Of the two kinds of rewards, the internal seems to be clearly the more effective and lasting aid to attention.

5 Reading and marking a textbook chapter Preview and then read and mark a chapter from one of your textbooks. Follow the directions in 4 above.

6 Writing study notes on a textbook selection You have previewed and read and marked the material on "The Importance of Attention." Now prepare study notes by jotting down in the margin of the selection recall words to help you learn the key ideas in the material.

Or you may prepare study notes for the selection on a separate sheet of paper. (You might want to review the guidelines and sample study notes on pages 53 to 55.) Your study notes should include main and key supporting points, enumerations, and definitions. Remember: Your purpose in taking study notes is to reduce a large quantity of information to the most important points. Include the items above, but do not overdevelop your notes or use too many outlining symbols. Express key points in the fewest words possible while still keeping the ideas complete and clear. Finally, after you complete the notes, don't forget to enter recall words in the margins of your notes.

7 Writing study notes on a textbook chapter You have previewed and read and marked the chapter from one of your textbooks. Now prepare study notes for the selection on a separate sheet of paper. (Give the name of the textbook, the author, and the chapter title at the top of the first sheet of study notes.) Follow the suggestions given in 6 above.

8 Reciting study notes on a textbook selection Use the technique of repeated self-testing to master your study notes on "The Importance of Attention." Convert the recall words written in the margin of your text or study notes into questions and recite the material until you can repeat it without looking at your notes. Then go on to the next recall word and repeat the same process. When you have mastered that material, go back and test yourself again on the first and then the second recall word. Continue until you review and master all the material.

9 Reciting study notes on a textbook chapter Use the technique of repeated self-testing to master the material in the study notes you took from one of your own textbook chapters. Follow the directions given above in 8.

10 Read the following description of one student's study situation:

> For his Western Civilization test tomorrow, Gary has to know three chapters from the text. At 1:30 yesterday afternoon, he sat down with a yellow marking pen and started reading the first chapter. At 3:00 he wasn't even halfway through the first chapter, and he felt bored and

worn out. The sentences were long and heavy and loaded with details. His head became so packed with information that as soon as he read a new idea, it seemed to automatically push out the one before it. When he looked back at what he had covered, he realized he had set off most of the text in yellow. He decided to stop marking and just read. But the more he read, the sleepier he got, and the more his mind kept wandering. He kept thinking about all the things he wanted to do once the test was over. At 5:15 he finished the first chapter but felt completely defeated. He still had to study the chapter, and he had no idea exactly what to study. On top of that, he had to plow through two more chapters and study them as well. He felt desperate and stupid— because he had waited so long to start with the text and because he was having such a hard time reading the chapters.

Now write a one-page (or longer) essay in which you answer *in detail* the question, "What can Gary do to read and study his textbook effectively?" Apply the information you have learned in this chapter.

5

Reading and Studying
Textbooks II:
Key Reading Skills

This chapter will improve your reading comprehension by helping you recognize:

- Definitions and examples

- Enumerations

- Headings and subheadings

- Signal words

- Main ideas in paragraphs and short selections

Perhaps you believe, as some students do, that reading comprehension should happen all at once. You may think that a single reading of a textbook selection should give you a satisfactory understanding of the material. But it's important to realize that good comprehension is usually a *process*. Very often comprehension is achieved gradually, as you move from perhaps a general feeling about what something means to a deeper level of understanding. The purpose of this chapter is to help you learn five key skills that will increase your understanding of what you read. You will learn how to recognize the following:

1. Definitions and examples
2. Enumerations (items in a list)
3. Headings and subheadings and relationships between them
4. Signal words
5. Main ideas in paragraphs and short selections

Having these skills will make it easier for you to use the approaches described in the previous chapter for reading and studying assigned material.

SKILL 1 RECOGNIZING DEFINITIONS AND EXAMPLES

Definitions are among the most important ideas in a selection. Definitions are particularly significant in introductory courses, where much of your time is spent mastering the specialized vocabulary of the subject. You are, in a sense, learning the "language" of sociology or biology or whatever the subject might be.

Most definitions are abstract, and so they are usually followed by one or more examples that clarify their meaning. Always select and mark off at least one example that makes an abstract definition clear for you.

In the following passage from a sociology textbook, underline the definition and write *Def* in the right-hand margin. Also, locate the two examples and write *Ex* in the right-hand margin beside each of them.

INTUITION

Galen, a famous Greek physician of the second century, prepared an elaborate chart of the human body showing exactly where it might be pierced without fatal injury. How did he know the vulnerable spots? He just knew them. True, he had learned a good deal of human anatomy through his observations and those of his associates; but beyond this, he relied upon his intuition to tell him which zones were fatal. Intuition is any flash of insight (true or mistaken) whose source the receiver cannot fully identify or explain. Hitler relied heavily upon his intuition, much to the distress of his generals. His intuition told him that France would not fight for the Rhineland, that England would not fight for Czechoslovakia, that England and France would not fight for Poland, and that England and France would quit when he attacked Russia. He was right on the first two insights and wrong on the last two.

You probably realized that the first lines of the passage are not the definition of intuition but an example. The definition ("Intuition is any flash or insight . . . .") is found midway through the paragraph. The examples (on Galen and Hitler) may be found at the beginning and end of the paragraph. Underlining the definition and putting *Ex* in the margin besides the examples will be helpful later when taking study notes on the passage.

• Activities on definitions and examples begin on page 73.

SKILL 2   RECOGNIZING ENUMERATIONS

Like definitions, enumerations are keys to important ideas. Enumerations are lists of items that may actually be numbered in the text. More often, however, a list of items is signaled by such words as *first of all, second, moreover, next, also, finally,* and others. Typical phrases that introduce enumerations are: "There are three reasons why . . ."; "The two causes of . . ."; "Five characteristics of . . ."; "There are several ways to . . ."; and so on.

In the selection below, number 1, 2, and 3 the disadvantages that going steady can have for young people. Note that each of the disadvantages will be indicated by a signal word.

From a psychological point of view, going steady long before one is ready to think seriously about marriage has several disadvantages. First, going steady prevents a person from learning about different types of individuals of the opposite sex. The girl who has dated boys who differ widely in intelligence, flexibility, mood, and other personality characteristics is in a far better position to select a suitable marriage partner than the girl who has gone out with only one or two boys all her life.

Another difficulty with going steady is that it often leads to early marriage. Since early marriages tend to lead to a disproportionate number of divorces, going steady early in adolescence should be discouraged. Still another problem with going steady is that it increases the possibility of sexual involvement, a situation many adolescents are not prepared to deal with. For example, studies indicate that most unwed mothers in their teens were going steady when they got pregnant.

You should have put a 1 in front of "prevents learning about different types of individuals of the opposite sex" (signaled by "First"), a 2 in front of "often leads to early marriage" (signaled by "Another difficulty"), and 3 in front of "increases the possibility of sexual involvement" (signaled by "Still another problem"). Develop the habit of looking for and numbering all the enumerations in a chapter.

When you take study notes on enumerations, be sure to include a heading that explains what a list is about. For example, because the list below does not have a descriptive heading, the notes are not clear:

1. Prevents a person from learning about different types of individuals of opposite sex
2. Often leads to early marriage
3. Increases the possibility of sexual involvement

On the other hand, your notes would be clear and helpful if they included, as do the notes below, a heading describing what the list is about:

Disadvantages of Going Steady Too Soon

1. Prevents a person from learning about different types of individuals of the opposite sex
2. Often leads to early marriage
3. Increases the possibility of sexual involvement

• Activities on enumerations begin on page 75.

SKILL 3   RECOGNIZING HEADINGS AND SUBHEADINGS

Authors use headings and subheadings to signal main ideas and to indicate the relationships among key points. Main heads are usually in larger typeface; they also may be set off by capital letters or different color ink. Subheadings are usually in smaller type; they may be underlined, italicized, or set in from the margin.

There are two methods for using headings and subheadings to locate key ideas. Each method is explained and illustrated below.

Method 1

Change a heading into one or more basic questions.   Then when you read the selection, do so partly with the purpose of finding the answer(s) to the question(s). Consider, for example, the following textbook selection:

DECLINE OF THE PURITAN WORK ETHIC

The Puritan concept of work as necessary for survival and as a duty and virtue in and of itself long dominated our culture. Work, obedience, thrift, and the delay of gratification were valued highly, and people's righteousness was often judged according to how hard they worked and how much they accomplished.

These views have changed, however, at an accelerated pace. Today's workers, particularly young workers, demand much more of themselves and their job than simply "filling a slot" and earning a living. The search for a meaningful, fulfilling job has become crucial. Workers increasingly desire to have responsibility and autonomy, to have a voice, and to demand not merely good physical working conditions but also good psychological working conditions. Rigid, authoritarian work structures are increasingly rejected as workers look to their jobs as a significant source of creative self-expression.

The title could be changed into the two basic questions: "What is the Puritan work ethic?" "Why has the Puritan work ethic declined?" The answer to the second question especially (the Puritan work ethic has declined because today's workers want meaningful, personally fulfilling jobs) forms the main idea of the passage. This technique of turning headings into basic questions often helps you cut through a mass of words to get to the heart of the matter. Develop the habit of using such questions to steer yourself to main ideas.

Method 2

Determine how subheads, if they follow a main head, are related to the main head. For example, suppose you noted the following main head and subheads spaced out over three pages of a business text:

ADVANTAGES OF THE PRIVATE ENTERPRISE SYSTEM

Freedom of Choice by Consumers
Decentralized Decision Making
High Productivity

Without having read a word of the text, you will have found one of the main ideas of these pages: The private enterprise system has the three advantages of (1) freedom of choice by consumers, (2) decentralized decision making, and (3) high productivity.

Often the relationship between headings and subheads will be as clear and direct as in this example. Other times, however, you must read or think a bit to see how a heading and its subheads relate. For instance, in a psychology text, following the main head DEFENSE MECHANISMS are the subheads *Rationalization, Projection, Repression, Identification, Reaction Formation,* and *Substitution.* When you realize that the subheads are different *kinds* of defense mechanisms, you have found one of the most important ideas on those pages—without having read even a word of the text. Sometimes there will be no clear relationship between the heading and subheads. You want to be ready, though, to take advantage of a relationship when it is present.

- Activities on headings and subheadings begin on page 76.

SKILL 4 RECOGNIZING SIGNAL WORDS

Signal words help you, the reader, follow the direction of a writer's thought. They are like signposts on the road that guide the traveler. Common signal words show emphasis, addition, change of direction, and illustration.

1 **Emphasis signals**   One way authors emphasize words or ideas is by setting them off in italic or boldface type, special type that looks *like this* or **like this.** Italics and boldface tell you that certain ideas are important.

Authors also signal important ideas by using words that show emphasis. Look over the list below which contains some typical words signaling emphasis.

above all	most effective
the chief outcome	most noteworthy
a central issue	most of all
the chief factor	the most substantial issue
especially valuable	pay particular attention to
important to note	a primary concern
a key feature	remember that
a major event	should be noted
the main value	a significant factor

Now read the paragraph below and circle the emphasis words.

The most effective solution to the various approaches to sex education is a course of compromise. Clear information about the physiological and psychological aspects of sex should be presented to students. Above all, however, students must be encouraged to view sexuality within the Judeo-Christian framework. They must be helped to become sensitive, responsible sexual beings.

You should have circled *most effective solution* and *Above all.*

2   **Addition signals**   Addition words tell you the writer's ideas are going to continue in the same direction and that the writer plans to add on more points or details. Look over the following addition words.

also	first of all	last of all	one
another	for one thing	likewise	another
finally	furthermore	moreover	second
first	in addition	next	the third reason

Now read the selection below and circle the major addition words.

Despite favorable surface conditions, there were throughout the 1920s defects in the American economy. First, some major industries did not experience the general prosperity which characterized most of the economy. Meager farm income meant that farmers lacked purchasing power to buy their share of the increasing output of goods and services. Coal, textiles, and shoes were among other industries which suffered from low profit margins. Moreover, while employment rose during the 1920s, the biggest gains were in the low-paid service trades rather than in those industries where earnings were high. Furthermore, the condition of American foreign trade was not as healthy as it appeared.

You should have circled the addition words *First, Moreover,* and *Furthermore.*

3   **Change-of-direction signals**   Change-of-direction words show that writer will probably reverse or modify a previous statement. Look over the following change-of-direction words.

but	in contrast	on the other hand
conversely	instead	otherwise
even though	nevertheless	still
however	on the contrary	yet

Now read the selection below and circle the change-of-direction words.

Everyone knows that infants sleep more than children, and children more than adults. However, it is less well known that no one single standard can be set as normal for adults. Most persons feel that about seven or eight hours is right for them. But a few may need as little as four hours a night, and others as much as eleven to twelve hours.

You should have circled the change-of-direction words *However* and *But.*

4 **Illustration signals** Writers use illustration words to signal that an example will be given to make an idea clear. Look over the following list of illustration words.

for example	once	such as
for instance	specifically	to illustrate

Now read the selection below and circle the illustration words.

The situations that trigger fear in the first year of human life are quite predictable. Specifically, in the infant and young child, unlearned fears are caused primarily by strange situations that are sudden or unexpected. A loud noise, for example, does not necessarily elicit fear in babies or small children, but if it comes suddenly, they will usually cry out in startled fright.

You should have circled *Specifically* and *for example.*

- Activities on signal words begin on page 79.

SKILL 5 RECOGNIZING MAIN IDEAS IN PARAGRAPHS

Learning to identify the main idea in textbook paragraphs is a key step in increasing your reading comprehension. Many paragraphs develop a central thought. That key idea is usually expressed in one sentence called a *main-idea sentence* (or *topic sentence*). The other sentences in the paragraph contain specific details that support or develop the main-idea sentence. The main idea is often, but not always, located in the first sentence of a paragraph.

To find the main idea, look for a general statement. Then ask yourself the question, *"Does all or most of the material in the paragraph develop or support the idea in this statement?"* Read the following paragraph, looking for the main-idea sentence. Then, to test if the sentence expresses the main thought of the paragraph, ask yourself the italicized question above. Enclose in brackets what you decide is the main idea.

The Dawes Act, nevertheless, did the Indians little but harm. In dividing the land as the act provided, the government usually gave the poorest territory to the Indians; the best was sold to white settlers. Even where individual Indians obtained good land, inexperience with legal matters left them vulnerable to the same kind of sharp practice that had marked the making of tribal treaties. Again and again, braves were tricked into selling their best holdings. More disastrous still, they had neither the tradition nor the incentive to cultivate the land they retained. Many became paupers. The few exceptions included the handful of Indians who held onto their oil-rich Oklahoma lands and became millionaires.

You were correct if you decided that the general idea appears in the first sentence, "The Dawes Act, nevertheless, did the Indians little but harm." You should have tested this idea by seeing whether the rest of the sentences in the paragraph support or develop this main idea. In fact, the paragraph gives three examples of the problem Indians had. First, they were usually given the poorest land. Second, because they were not knowledgeable about legal matters, they were often tricked into selling good land. And finally, they didn't always have the skills needed to tend the land.

Now read the paragraph below and enclose in brackets the main-idea sentence. Remember: The main idea of a paragraph isn't always expressed in the first sentence.

The very idea of a fire in a crowded building is enough to frighten most people. And with good reason: all too often, the cry "Fire!" causes people to stampede to the nearest exit, trampling each other on the way. Fear seems to break down normal rational behavior. The result is unnecessary injury. Research studies have duplicated this panic behavior. In one experiment, several people were given a string to hold; each string was attached to a spool placed inside a bottle. The bottle neck was large enough for only one spool at a time to be removed. Told to get their spools out before the bottle filled with water, all the people tried to remove their spools at the same time. The resulting traffic jam kept everyone from getting the spools out in time. Even worse jams were produced by the experimenters when they threatened their subjects with electric shocks if they did not get their spools out before the bottle filled.

You were correct if you decided that the general idea appears in the third sentence, "Fear seems to break down normal rational behavior." You should have tested the idea by seeing whether the rest of the sentence in the paragraph support and develop this idea. In fact, the paragraph gives two examples of how fear can break down rational behavior. The first example is that the cry of "Fire" in a building often causes people to stampede to the exits. The second extended example describes an experiment in which people panic when confronted by an artificial but still frightening situation.

If initially you decided that the first sentence was the main idea of the paragraph, you would not have found any support in the rest of the paragraph for the sentence. Remember: Test what you think is the main idea by asking yourself if the rest of the paragraph develops the idea.

• Activities on the main idea begin on page 80.

Activities

1   Review the chapter carefully. Then, without looking back, answer the following questions.

   1. True or false: _____ Very often, reading comprehension is a process that is achieved gradually rather than something that happens all at once.

   2. Definitions should be set off by underlining them and writing _____ in the margin; examples should be set off by writing _____ in the margin.

   3. Main heads may be set off from subheads by:
      a. Larger typeface   d. Different color ink
      b. Capital letters   e. All of the above
      c. Spacing

   4. Circle the two methods of using headings and subheadings to locate main ideas:
      a. Change a head into one or more basic questions.
      b. Number all the heads and subheads in the selection.
      c. Determine how subheads that follow a main head are related to the main head.
      d. Underline the words in the heads and subheads whenever they appear in the text.

   5. When you take notes on an enumeration, always include a _____ that explains what the list is about.

2   **Locating definitions and examples**   Read quickly through the following selections, underlining each definition and writing *Ex* in the left-hand margin beside an example of the definition. Some definitions will have several examples, but you need mark off only one example that makes the definition clear for you.

    Note that textbook authors often call attention to terms they are defining by setting them off in italic type.

   1. *Territoriality* refers to persons' assumptions that they have exclusive rights to certain geographic areas, even if these areas are not theirs by legal right. To take a common example, by the end of the first week of class, most students consider a particular seat to be their territory and will show signs of distress or irritation if someone else sits in that seat. What is interesting, even from the simple example we cited, are the subtle ways in which strangers observe certain implicit territorial rights and the emotional mechanisms that regulate this behavior. We shall return to this in a moment.

Personal space refers not to a geographic area but to the space surrounding our body, a space that moves with us. Persons regard that space as private and try to prevent others from entering it. For example, persons sitting in a public reading room definitely seek to have at least one empty seat between themselves and the next reader. The phenomenon is also evident in less formal settings.

2. Energy is the capacity of matter to do work. In this respect, matter can have both potential and kinetic energy. Potential energy is stored-up energy or energy an object possesses due to its relative position. For example, a ball located 20 feet above the ground has more potential energy than another ball located 10 feet above the ground, and will bounce higher when allowed to fall. Water backed up behind a dam represents potential energy that can be converted into useful work in the form of electrical energy. Gasoline represents a source of stored-up chemical potential energy that can be released during combustion.

   Kinetic energy is the energy that matter possesses due to its motion. When the water behind the dam is released and allowed to flow, its potential energy is changed into kinetic energy, which may be used to drive generators and produce electricity. All moving bodies possess kinetic energy. The pressure exerted by a confined gas is due to the kinetic energy of rapidly moving gas particles. We all know the results when two moving vehicles collide—their kinetic energy is expended in the "crash" that occurs.

3. The fact that you have been going to school for so many years indicates society's faith in transfer of training, namely, that what you learn in your courses will be useful later. There are two fundamentally different types of transfer, positive and negative. Suppose I have learned that in order to keep the attention of my class in introductory psychology, I must tell a joke every 10 minutes or so. It seems to be a reasonably successful device, so I also try it in my class in personality psychology, and it works there too. This is an example of *positive transfer:* What I have learned to do in one situation applies equally well in another situation. But suppose that I try to carry it one step further and use the technique in a talk that I give at the faculty club. Here I discover that my jokes fall flat and the talk is a failure. This is an example of *negative transfer:* What worked in one situation was not applicable to another situation.

3   Locating definitions and examples in a textbook   Using a chapter or chapters in one of your textbooks, find five definitions and examples. Choose only definitions for which there are examples. Also, make sure each example is one that helps make the meaning of a definition clear to you. Write the definitions and their examples on a sheet of paper. At the top of the paper, give the name of the textbook, the author(s), the chapter title(s), and the pages of the textbook you are using. Your instructor might want to refer to the text when reviewing your answers.

4 Locating enumerations In the selection below, number 1, 2, 3, etc., the items in each list or enumeration. Remember that words such as *first, another, also,* and *finally* often signal an enumeration. Also, in the space provided write a heading that explains what each list is about.

1. Heading _____

There are two basic forms of immaturity. One is called fixation, in which a person remains emotionally at an earlier level of development. A fixated person is one who has never outgrown certain childish attitudes, ideas, or behaviors. The other type is called regression, a return to an earlier level of maturity. Many people show signs of regression temporarily while they are under stress. Some examples of their behavior during difficult periods might include pouting or throwing temper tantrums. During regression, people display behavior patterns that are more characteristic of children than of adults.

2. Heading _____

If Congress lost some of its momentum during 1966, it wrote a proud record of accomplishment nevertheless. First, it created the Department of Transportation as the twelfth department in the Cabinet, giving it full responsibility for the development of a coordinated national transportation system. It passed a $1.2 billion "demonstration cities" program to create models for urban development. For the first time in history, it established safety standards for all highway vehicles. It broadened the regulations for the labeling and packaging of foods, drugs, cosmetics, and household supplies. Finally, Congress appropriated $3.7 billion to help clean up the country's rivers and lakes and $186 million to fight air pollution.

3. Heading _____

We have defined directed thinking as being aimed at the solution to a specific problem, and logical thinking as one method of getting to such a solution. But in concrete terms, what are the actual steps we go through when we have a complex problem to solve?

It is first necessary to *identify* the problem—to know that it exists and then to pinpoint and delineate it in order to see how you will direct your thinking to solve it. You first become aware of a problem as an obstacle or frustration—not always an unpleasant one, certainly, or sports and puzzles would not exist. Say you have just made a date to play tennis. After hanging up the phone, you realize that you have a dental appointment for exactly the same time. The problem is now identified: you are committed to being at two different places at 1:30 tomorrow afternoon.

After this, you begin to *search* for possible solutions. With some problems this search can be as simple as random trial and error, like fitting one key after another into a lock until you find the one that works. If you stumble upon the right solution by the trial-and-error method, of course, you need go no further. But many problems do not yield to such a mechanical solution, and trying every possible alternative is not a very economical approach. Still, to some extent, trial and error probably does enter into your search for a solution. First you start restricting your alternatives. Can you simply not turn up at the dentist's? No. Not show up at the tennis court? Not a good idea, either. Perhaps you had better call your friend back. Next, you *analyze* the situation: if you explain to your friend what the difficulty is, maybe you can work out another time for the tennis game.

You then move to the *attack* itself. You telephone your friend, and you agree to meet on the courts at 4:00 instead of 1:30. You no longer have to be in two places at once, and your problem is solved.

Sometimes, of course, the interval between the appearance of a problem and its solution is short enough that you think of it as all having happened in a single step. What has really happened is that these four steps have occurred so rapidly that the solution seemed to come instantaneously. Other times—if the problem is a very complicated one, such as finding a cure for cancer—the single problem must be broken down into many parts, and the steps must be gone through, over and over, by many people.

5   Locating enumerations in a textbook   Using one of your textbooks, find and record five separate enumerations. Write a heading for each list. There should be at least three items under each heading.

At the top of the first sheet of paper on which you do this activity, give the name of the textbook you are using, the author(s), and the pages.

6   Turning headings into basic questions   The following are headings taken from a variety of college texts. Change each heading into one or more *meaningful* basic questions, using words like *What, Why, Who, Which, When, In what ways, How*. For example, the head "Alternatives to Conflict" could be turned into the basic question, "What are alternatives to conflict?" "Which is the best alternative?"

Use a separate sheet of paper for this activity.

The War of 1812	Heredity and Development
The Dark Ages and the Glimmer of Light	Pollution and Business
	Characteristics of Living Things
Taft-Hartley Act	The Two Terms of Theodore
Coping with Frustration	Roosevelt
The Social Dropouts	Heart Disease

7   Locating answers to basic questions about main heads   Read the following selections to find the answer to the basic question or questions asked. Write your answer(s) in the space provided.

1. Question: Who is on the Council of Economic Advisors?

THE COUNCIL OF ECONOMIC ADVISORS
The President is assisted in economic matters by a Council of Economic
Advisors, which consists of three members appointed by him and
approved by the Senate. These three council members are professional economists who analyze and interpret economic development
and recommend national economic policy to the President. The
council was created by the Congress with the passage of the
Employment Act of 1946.

Answer: _____

_____

2. Questions: What are the speaker's resources? Which is the
speaker's most important resource?

THE SPEAKER'S RESOURCES
People planning to make a speech on any subject have just two
resources: what they know and what they can find out. Each one bears
a familiar label. The first is thinking, the second is investigating. We
labor the distinction for the very good reason that students so often
do not. More than five hundred students were asked, "How do you
prepare your speeches?" Over half said the first thing they did was
to look for speech material in the library! Does this support Thomas
Edision's cryptic comment that "there is nothing to which men will not
resort in order to avoid the labor of thinking"? Running to the
library and to the *Readers' Guide* or to an encyclopedia means that
you end up looking first for what other people know about your
subject. But it is your subject. What do *you* know?

Answers: _____

_____

3. Questions: Who created the Peace Corps? Why was the Peace
Corps created?

THE PEACE CORPS
In the hope of winning back some of the friends the United States
had alienated by the Bay of Pigs invasion, in September of 1961
President Kennedy created the Peace Corps, one of the most popular
measures of his administration. The Peace Corps was composed of
Americans of all ages who volunteered to work for token wages in
virtually every nation outside the Communist bloc. Their task was to
teach and to work with native citizens of the country in any way that
would be of help. More than 3,000 men and women, many of them
idealistic young people, flocked to join the Peace Corps, which was
directed by President Kennedy's brother-in-law Sargent Shriver. Their

work and that of thousands of additional volunteers elicited an almost uniformly favorable response throughout the world and contributed significantly to restoring American prestige on the international scene.

Answers: _____

_____

8   Turning headings into basic questions   Using a chapter from one of your textbooks, change five headings into basic questions. Then read the sections under the headings to find accurate and concise answers to the questions.

On a separate sheet of paper, indicate the headings, the question(s) you ask about the headings, and the answers to the question(s). At the top of the first sheet on which you do this activity, give the name of the textbook, the author(s), and the pages.

9   Locating relationships between main heads and subheads Probably all your textbooks contain main heads and subheads that have a clear relationship to each other. The main head and subheads in the following example are taken from a college sociology text:

Textbook	*Sociology*
Author(s)	*Horton and Hunt* *Page(s) 366—368*
Main head	*Characteristics of Crowd Behavior*
Subheads	*1. Anonymity* *3. Suggestibility*
	2. Impersonality *4. Social Contagion*

Following the main head "Characteristics of Crowd Behavior" are four subheads, titles in smaller print under the main heading. Each subhead, it is clear, is one of the characteristics of crowd behavior. By recognizing the relationship between the main head and the subheads, the reader has found an important idea—without having yet read a word of the text!

Using one of your textbooks, list on a separate sheet of paper five main heads and subheads that have a clear relationship to each other. Be sure to *number* the subheads and to find a minimum of two subheads in each case. Also, include the numbers of the pages on which you find your main heads and subheads in case your instructor wants to refer to the text in reviewing your answers.

10 Identifying common types of signal words Below are some of the signal words often used by writers. Place each word under its proper heading.

for example	yet	most significant
moreover	also	however
most important	another	such as
but	for instance	especially valuable

Emphasis signals   **Addition signals**

_____   _____

_____   _____

_____   _____

Illustration signals   **Change-of-direction signals**

_____   _____

_____   _____

_____   _____

11 Locating signal words Circle all the signal words in the selections that follow. Your instructor may or may not ask you to write in the margin beside each word whether it is an emphasis, addition, change-of-direction, or illustration signal.

1. One of the oldest and most persistent desires of human beings has been to indulge in mood-changing and pleasure-giving practices. For instance, diverse cultures have engaged in the drinking of alcoholic beverages of all descriptions. But as with most pleasures, over-indulgence can be harmful to oneself and others. Also, not everyone agrees that drinking or using other mood modifiers should be an accepted pleasure.

2. Energy is used to cause chemical changes. For example, a chemical change occurs in the electroplating of metals when electrical energy is passed through a salt solution in which the metal is submerged. A chemical change also occurs when radiant energy from the sun is utilized by plants in the process of photosynthesis. Moreover, as we saw, a chemical change occurs when heat causes mercuric oxide to decompose. Chemical changes are often used to produce energy rather than new substances. The heat or thrust generated during the combustion of fuels is more important than the products formed.

3. A major goal in group encounter is that people come to know each other better emotionally. Positive feelings emerge, and previously

unloved, lonely people may begin to experience positive regard from others in the group. The path to this goal is difficult, however. The expression of negative feelings and aggression may be upsetting; the breaking down of facades is likely to result in a weakening of defenses against anxiety. Another difficulty is that increased freedom of expression developed within the group may make people outside the group uncomfortable; for example, a husband or wife who is not in the group may not share and so not welcome this new emotional freedom.

12 Identifying main ideas Under each of the following paragraphs are four general statements. Decide which statement best expresses the main idea of the paragraph. Circle the letter of that statement. Remember that all or most of the material in the paragraph should develop the statement you choose.

1. Of late the drug methadone is being used in some treatment programs for heroin addicts. Methadone has some advantages over heroin. It is cheap and it usually does not produce strong euphoria. It can be used as an effective substitute for heroin, and the heroin addict substituting methadone is not reduced to theft or prostitution. However, methadone is addictive. And the long-term symptoms associated with methadone are similar to those associated with heroin: constipation and loss of appetite. Heroin addicts who substitute methadone are still addicts. They have been helped, not cured. But perhaps in some instances this limited goal is the only practical one.

   a. Methadone has some advantages over heroin.
   b. Methadone has both advantages and disadvantages.
   c. Methadone is addictive.
   d. The long-term symptoms of methadone resemble heroin symptoms.

2. Meanwhile, factory and automobile pollution increased. Rivers turned into stinking sewers from industrial wastes; fish and plant life in lakes died; and city populations choked and gasped in smog. A series of rocket expeditions to the moon began in 1969, but many asked in mounting cynicism how a nation so afflicted with grave problems at home could continue spending astronomical sums on such exploits. Fueled by the panic of growing numbers of drug addicts for money, crime rates soared. Entire sections of great cities displayed empty sidewalks at night, the residents hidden behind locked doors and windows, which often were broken in by burglars. Candidates for political office could ride to victory on the law-and-order issue almost by itself. Twisting and warping every other problem, and producing massive protest and disillusionment, was the seemingly endless war in Vietnam.

    a. Pollution and crime were on the increase in the United States.
    b. Many began to question the country's priorities.
    c. The Vietnam war was responsible for a growing number of problems in the United States.
    d. Conditions in the United States grew worse.

3. The deterioration of the earth's environment is the result of the impact of each individual on the environment multiplied by the number of individuals. Suppose you could choose any life-style you wished. You could, for example, choose to be a Buddhist monk or nun. You would be forbidden to have money, and the only food you would be allowed to eat would be that placed in your begging bowl by the pious. You would own your begging bowl, a robe, a needle and thread, and that is all. Your presence on earth would cause very little deterioration of the environment. On the other hand, you could choose to be an American millionaire. You would own several houses and have numerous automobiles and perhaps a jet plane. You might own several polluting factories and have a half dozen children, all eventually with their own houses, cars, and polluting factories. It is obvious that you would contribute much more to environmental deterioration than the Buddhist monk or nun.

    a. The life-style that you choose determines your environmental impact.
    b. As a beggar, you would add little pollution to the environment.
    c. People should choose a personally rewarding life-style.
    d. A millionaire is capable of heavy pollution of the environment.

13 Locating main ideas Put brackets around the main idea in each of the paragraphs that follow. The paragraphs are taken from a variety of articles and college textbooks.

To find the main idea, look for a general statement. Then ask yourself, "Does all or most of the material in the paragraph develop or support the idea in this statement?"

1. During the Depression, money shortages produced important changes in the daily lives of people. Car owners often ran their automobiles until they simply defied repair. Children's college educations were postponed because parents could not pay even modest tuition charges of less than $100 in state-supported institutions. Trips to the doctor and dentist were delayed until a major emergency forced a family to seek medical attention. Even with federal food distribution after 1933, millions of families had inadequate diets. What made the lack of money and resulting poverty tolerable was that the condition was so widespread.

2. Toys are an integral part of children's play worlds. When purchasing toys, parents should resist the impulse to buy something which appeals to them and concentrate on buying toys that are suitable for the child. Infants profit most from toys they can look at and feel, chew on, hold, and drop. Naturally, such toys must be large enough so that they cannot be swallowed. One- to two-year-olds enjoy toys that they can take apart and put together and toys that they can pull and push. For young children, educational toys which give youngsters a chance to learn different textures and colors and help them learn number concepts are good. Nontoxic modeling clay, vegetable dye paints, construction sets, and dolls that can be dressed and changed are all valuable toys. For four- and five-year-olds, toys which help with manipulative skills and which stimulate coordination of physical and mental abilities are helpful.

3. People have often lamented what a waste it is that we spend a third of our lives asleep. Think what we must be missing! What we are actually missing by being able to sleep is the following: visual, auditory, and tactile sensory disorders; vivid hallucinations; inability to concentrate; withdrawal; disorientation of self, time, and place; lapses of attention; increased heart rate and stress hormones in the blood; and the onset of psychosis. This alarming list, of course, refers to extreme instances, in which, for example, people have stayed up, on a bet or for a television marathon, for upward of 200 hours. But if you have ever been up all night, you may fall asleep in class the next day and be slower in taking notes or answering questions on an exam. In short, the human body needs sleep to function, much as it needs food and water.

14 Locating main ideas in a textbook   In an article or textbook, locate five different paragraphs in which the main idea is clearly expressed in one sentence. Make copies of the paragraphs (there may be a duplicating machine in your library), put brackets around the main-idea sentences, and hand in the selections to your instructor.

6

Training Your Memory

This chapter will show you how to develop your memory by:

• Organizing the material to be learned

• Intending to remember

• Testing yourself repeatedly

• Spacing memory work over several sessions

• Using study periods and pre-exam time most efficiently

Perhaps you feel that memorizing material for a test is a waste of time; you may be convinced that you will forget what you memorize as soon as a test is over. Moreover, because some teachers feel that memorization and learning are incompatible, they may tell you that you shouldn't *memorize* material; rather, you should *understand* it.

Memorization, however, can be an important aid to understanding—and not just in situations where basic, uncomplicated material is involved. Effective memorizing requires that you organize and repeatedly test yourself on the material to be learned. As you do this, you are sure to enlarge your comprehension of the material and notice relationships you had not seen before. In short, memorization and understanding *reinforce* one another. Together, they help you learn—and learning is the goal of education. What you need, then, is a series of strategies or steps to help you memorize effectively. The following pages present six such steps:

1. Organize the material to be learned.
2. Intend to remember.
3. Test yourself repeatedly on the material to be memorized.
4. Space memory work over several sessions.
5. Use as a study period the time just before going to bed.
6. Jot down on exams key words, catch words, and catch phrases.

STEP 1   ORGANIZE THE MATERIAL TO BE LEARNED

Perhaps you have tried to memorize material without first organizing it. For example, you may have picked out definitions in a textbook chapter and tried to memorize them without having read the whole chapter. Or you may have missed several lectures and tried to catch up on all that happened by memorizing a friend's notes, even though you had no overall sense of what the classes had covered. In both cases, you probably did not understand the material and so had trouble memorizing it. What you tried to do was commit to memory isolated bits and pieces of information; you had no real understanding of how the pieces fit together. To avoid this trap, be sure to prepare organized study notes of textbook and class material *before* you try to memorize that information. (See pages 30 and 51 for suggestions on taking study notes.)

STEP 2   INTEND TO REMEMBER

If you want to memorize material, you must actively decide to remember it. *Your attitude is crucial!* This advice seems so obvious that many people overlook its value. But if you make the decision to remember something and you then work at mastering it, you *will* remember.

Most of us tend to forget the names of people to whom we are introduced. We forget because we never really intended to remember. However, if we *had to* recall a person's name (suppose, for example, that we lent that person money), our intention would change and, not surprisingly, we would remember. All of us can have a beartrap memory—if we work at it.

STEP 3   TEST YOURSELF REPEATEDLY ON THE MATERIAL TO BE LEARNED

After you have organized the material you intend to learn, memorize it through repeated self-testing. Look at the first item in your notes; then look away and try to repeat it to yourself. When you can, look at the next item; look away and try to repeat it. When you can repeat the second item, *go back* without looking at your notes and repeat the first and second items. After you can recall the first two items without referring to your notes, go on to the third item, and so on. In short, follow this procedure: *After you learn each new item, go back and test yourself on all the previous items. This constant review is at the heart of self-testing* and is the key to effective memorization.

The following techniques will help you in the self-testing process:

1. Use several senses
2. Use key words
3. Use catch words
4. Use catch phrases

Each technique is explained and illustrated on the pages ahead.

Use Several Senses

Use several senses in the self-testing process. Studies have shown that most people understand and retain information more effectively when several senses are involved in learning the material. Do not, then, merely recite the information silently to yourself. Also repeat it out loud so that you *hear* it, and write it down so that you *see* it. These steps will help you learn more than if you only repeated the information silently to yourself.

Use Key Words

Key words can be used as "hooks" to help you remember ideas. A key word stands for an idea and is so central to the idea that if you remember the word, you are almost sure to remember the entire concept that goes with the word.

Here is an illustration of how key words may function as hooks to help recall ideas. Assume that your biology instructor has announced that the class will be tested on a textbook chapter dealing with the ecology of urban life. This is one important paragraph taken from that chapter.

> Urban planners who want to replace living plants with plastic ones seem to think that the city does not need to have living plants in it. Actually, plants do many useful things in a city even if they are not producing food for people. Plants improve the quality of the air by giving off oxygen and woodsy-smelling compounds, such as those emitted by pine trees. Smog contains some gases that, in low concentrations, can be used as nutrients by plants. Thus plants can absorb some air pollutants. Evaporation of water from plants cools the air; also, the leaves of plants catch falling dust particles. Trees and shrubs muffle the noise of what otherwise could be the deafening sound of street traffic and construction work. Finally, the roots of plants—even weeds on vacant lots—help to hold earth in place and reduce the number of soil particles blown into the air and washed into sewers.

Since you want to learn this information, you would first prepare study notes that might look something like this:

Uses of Plants in City

1. Give off oxygen (and pleasant smell)
2. Absorb air pollutants (gases used as nutrients)
3. Cool the air (evaporation from leaves)
4. Catch dust particles
5. Muffle noises (traffic, construction)
6. Hold earth in place

One way to memorize these study notes is to use key words as hooks. What you do is circle a key word from each of the listed items. The word you select should help you pull into memory the entire idea which it represents. Write each of the words one after the other under the study notes. Here is how your notes would look.

Uses of Plants in City

1. Give off (oxygen) (and pleasant smell)
2. Absorb air (pollutants) (gases used as nutrients)

3. (Cool) the air (evaporation from leaves)
4. Catch (dust) particles
5. (Muffle) noises (traffic, construction)
6. Hold (earth) in place

Key words: oxygen, pollutants, cool, dust, muffle, earth

You would now test yourself repeatedly until you could remember each of the six key words and the concepts they stand for.

Use Catch Words

Sometimes people who use key words to pull central ideas into memory can't remember one of the key words and so they forget the entire concept the word represents. Using catch words is one way to ensure that you remember an entire series of key words and so the ideas they stand for.

Follow these guidelines when you prepare catch words. First, circle the key words in your study notes. Then write down the first letter of each key word. Here are the first letters for the key words in the paragraph about city plants: *O* (oxygen), *P* (pollutants), *C* (cool), *D* (dust), *M* (muffle) and *E* (earth). Now, if necessary, rearrange the letters to form an easily recalled catch word. It can be a real word or a nonsense word. For example, you might remember the letters O-P-C-D-M-E with the nonsense word MEDCOP.

What matters is that you create a word that you can automatically remember and that the letters in the word help you recall the key words (and so the ideas the key words represent).

After you create a catch word, test yourself until you are sure each letter stands for a key word in your mind. Here is how the catch word MEDCOP can be used to pull into memory the textbook paragraph about city plants:

MEDOCP

M = muffle
E = earth
D = dust
C = cool
O = oxygen
P = pollutants

Cover the key words (*muffle, earth,* etc.) with a sheet of paper, leaving only the first letter exposed. Look at the letter *M* and see if you can recall the key word *muffle* and the idea that plants muffle noise. Next, look at the letter *E* and see if you remember the key word *earth* and the idea that plant's roots hold the earth in place. Then do the same for the other four letters. In each case, the letter serves as a hook to pull into memory the key word and then the whole idea.

Use Catch Phrases

Another way to remember key words is to form some easily recalled catch phrase. Each word in the catch phrase begins with the first letter of a different key word. For example, suppose you had to remember the six uses of city plants in the exact order in which they are presented in the textbook paragraph (*Oxygen, Pollutants, Cool, Dust, Muffle, Earth*). You would write a six-word phrase with the first word beginning with *O*, the second with *P*, the third with *C*, and so on. Here is a catch phrase you might create to help remember the order of the six letters and the key words they stand for:

Our parents cook dinner most evenings.

Your catch phrase does not have to be a model of perfect grammar nor does it have to make perfect sense. All that matters is that you create a phrase (no matter how outrageous) which will stick in your head and which you will automatically remember.

Once you create a catch phrase, follow the testing process already described in the section on catch words (page 87). Note that the first letter of each word in the catch phrase pulls into memory a key word and the key word recalls an entire idea. For example, the *O* in *Our* recalls the key word *oxygen* and the idea that plants give off oxygen, the *P* in *parents* helps you remember the key word *pollutants* and the idea that plants absorb air pollutants, and so on.

- *Note:* The four techniques just described are valuable for learning more than the simplest kind of material. Before you can create key words, catch words, and catch phrases, you must organize and prepare study notes. This preliminary work helps you develop a general understanding of the material. Once you have this perspective, you can pull together and integrate a great deal of material by using key words, catch words, and catch phrases. The information will no longer be broken into isolated, unrelated bits. Instead, you may begin to see relationships, make comparisons, and perceive implications. You will, in short, be deepening your understanding of the material.

STEP 4   SPACE MEMORY WORK OVER SEVERAL SESSIONS

If you try to do a great deal of self-testing at any time, you may have trouble absorbing the material. Always try to spread out your memory work. For instance, three one-hour sessions will be more effective than one three-hour session.

Spacing memory over several time periods gives you a chance to review and lock in material you have studied in an earlier session but have begun to forget. Research shows that we forget a good deal of information right after studying it. However, review within a day reduces much of this memory loss. So try to review new material within twenty-four hours after you first study it. Then, if possible, several days later review again to make a third impression or "imprint" of the material in your head. If you work this consistently to retain ideas and details, they are not likely to escape you when you need them during an exam.

STEP 5   USE AS A STUDY PERIOD THE TIME JUST BEFORE GOING TO BED

Study thoroughly the material to be learned, using the techniques described. Then conduct a final review right before going to bed. Go to sleep without watching late night television or reading a book or magazine. Your mind will work through and absorb much of the material during the night. In the morning, get up a half hour earlier than usual so that you will have time to go over the material once again. This morning review will complete the process of fixing the material solidly in your memory.

STEP 6   JOT DOWN ON EXAMS KEY WORDS, CATCH WORDS, AND CATCH PHRASES

Be sure to read the whole exam once quickly before answering any item. If you see a question which calls for the material you have learned, immediately write down the appropriate key words, catch words, and catch sentences. That way you will not forget those points when you go to answer that question.

Activities

1 Review the chapter carefully. Then, without looking back, answer the following questions.

    1. The first step in effective remembering is to _____ the material to be learned.

    2. The best way to avoid passive studying is to:
       a. Study right before bed.
       b. Test yourself on the material to be learned.
       c. Copy several times the material to be learned.
       d. Review material in the morning.

    3. True or false: _____ Material is best studied in a single long session rather than spaced out over several sessions.

    4. When you memorize material, you attitude is crucial. You must _____ to remember.

    5. If you reduce ideas to key words and memorize the key words, they will often serve as _____ that will help you pull into memory the ideas.

2 All the following items could be obtained in a large drugstore. On separate paper, organize the list by grouping together items that have something in common.

Ban deodorant	Scope mouthwash
Daily newspaper	*Reader's Digest*
Kent cigarettes	Bic lighter
Colgate toothpaste	Joy dish detergent
Newsweek magazine	Muriel cigars
Dental floss	Dial soap
Tide detergent	Toothbrush

Now memorize the fourteen items in the order in which you have arranged them. Use the technique of repeated self-testing to learn your list.

3 An instructor in a psychology class described the following four techniques used in behavior therapy: (1) extinction, (2) imitation, (3) reinforcement, and (4) desensitization. Make up a catch word that will help you remember the four techniques.

4 The following six recommendations for easing colds were presented in a lecture on health care. Use a catch word or catch phrase to memorize the recommendations in any order.

Recommendations for Colds
1. Aspirin
2. Hot drinks
3. Vitamin C
4. Oral decongestant
5. Nose drops
6. Bed rest

5 Assume that an instructor wants you to learn the following five influences on a child's personality. The influences are listed in order of importance.

Influences on Children
1. Parents
2. Siblings (brothers and sisters)
3. Friends
4. Close relatives
5. Teachers

Use a catch phrase to memorize in sequence the five influences.

6 A psychology text explains Abraham Maslow's theory of basic human needs. The needs, in order of importance, are listed below.

Basic Human Needs
1. Psychological needs
2. Safety needs
3. Need for companionship
4. Esteem needs
5. Need for self-actualization
6. Need for knowledge
7. Need for beauty

Use a catch phrase to memorize in sequence these seven needs.

7 Read the following selection taken from a consumer information text. Then look over the study notes on the selection.

HOUSEHOLD BUDGET HINTS
Here are some household tips that may increase your chances of living within your household budget. First, if you have a dishwasher, stop it before the dry cycle. Instead of using this cycle, the one requiring the most electricity, open your dishwasher door and let the dishes air-dry.

Another hint is to try to cook entire meals at one time in your oven. Many foods with different cooking temperatures can be cooked together at the same temperature, with little loss in taste or nutritive value. Also, if you have a washer in your home, wash full loads. Save clothes until you are ready to do many at one time. And try to wash all your clothes on cold settings; tests indicate that most fabrics can be thoroughly cleaned with cold-water detergents. Next, when you go the grocery store, go with a list, and shop only for the items on the list. If you don't resist the urge to put extra items in your shopping cart, you may quickly double your bill. Finally, don't open doors unnecessarily. For example, don't stand with the refrigerator door open trying to decide what you want to eat. Decide before you open the door. Don't constantly peek in the oven door to check on how a roast is doing; use a meat thermometer and a timer instead. Don't keep a door of the house open for any longer than necessary when entering or leaving. You're likely to let too much outside air into the house, and your air conditioner or heater will have to work more as a result.

Study Notes

Household Budget Tips
1. Stop dishwasher before dry cycle
2. Cook entire meals at one time in oven
3. Do full clothing loads with cold water in washer
4. Buy only items on shopping list
5. Open refrigerator, oven, house doors only when needed

Pick out a key word for each of the five budget hints and then use a catch word or catch phrase to memorize the hints.

8   Read the following description of one student's study situation:

In two days, Steve will have a biology quiz in which he will have to write the definitions of ten terms that have been discussed in the course. As a study aid, the teacher has passed out a list of thirty terms that students should know thoroughly. Steve has gone through his class notes and textbook and copied down the definitions of the thirty terms. He tries to study the terms by reading them over and over, but he can't concentrate and merely keeps "reading words." He decides to write out each definition until he knows it. Hours later, he has written out ten definitions a number of times and is still not sure he will remember them. He begins to panic because he has spent so much time but gotten such meager results. He decides to play Russian roulette with the terms—to study just some of them and hope they are the ones that will be on the test.

Now write a one-page (or longer) essay in which you answer *in detail* the question: "How can Steve improve his memory techniques so that he can learn all thirty terms in a reasonable amount of time?" In your answer, apply the information you have learned in this chapter.

7

Taking Objective and
Essay Exams

This chapter will show you how to:

- **Prepare for and take an objective exam**

- **Prepare for an essay exam**

- **Write a good essay exam**

- **Cram when you have no other choice**

Do you tend to panic during objective or essay exams? Do you some-times forget what you have learned as soon as you sit down and start looking at the questions? Or are you one of those students who run out of time while taking exams? Have you ever, for example, looked at your watch and discovered that you had only seven minutes left to write an essay worth forty points?

"How," you're probably wondering, "can I avoid these problems?" The answer is simple. *Be well prepared.* That means you must go to class consistently, read the textbook and any other assigned material, take class and textbook notes, and study and at times memorize your notes. In short, you must start preparing for exams the first class of the semester. The pages that follow offer a series of practical suggestions to help you use your study time efficiently.*

WHAT TO STUDY

You will not always know beforehand if a scheduled exam will be an objective or an essay test (or a combination of both). To be prepared for whatever kind of test your instructor gives, you should, throughout the course, pay attention to the following:

1 Key terms, their definitions, and the examples that clarify the meaning of the terms (see also page 65). Look for this material in your class and textbook notes. If your textbook notes are not com-plete, go back to the original reading material to locate key terms. This information is often set off in *italics* or **boldface.**

2 Enumerations (list of items) found in your class and textbook notes (see also page 66). Often these enumerations are the basis of essay questions.

   Items in a list will probably have a descriptive heading—for example, the characteristics of living things, the major schools of contemporary psychology, the primary consequences of the Indus-trial Revolution—and the items should be numbered. Be sure to learn the heading that describes the list as well as the items in the list.

3 Points emphasized in class or in the text. Often words such as *the most significant, of special importance, the chief reason,* and so on

---

* *Note:* Many of the suggestions offered in this chapter assume that you know how to take effective classroom and textbook notes (Chapters 3 and 4) and that you know how to memorize such notes (Chapter 6). If you have not developed these essential skills, refer to the appropriate chapters.

(see page 69) are used to call attention to important points in a book or in a lecture. When you take notes on such material, mark these significant points with an *Imp,* asterisk (*), or other mark (such as }).

Also, as you go through your class notes, concentrate on areas the instructor spent a good deal of time discussing. For example, if the instructor spent a week talking about present-day changes in the traditional family structure, or the importance of the carbon atom, or the advantages of capitalism, or early key figures in the development of psychology as a science, you can reasonably expect to get a question on the emphasized area. Similarly, review your textbook. If many pages in a chapter deal with one area, you may be sure that subject is important and so you should expect a question about it on an exam.

4 Areas your instructors have advised you to study. Some instructors conduct in-class reviews during which they tell students what material to emphasize when they study. Always write down these pointers; your instructors have often made up the test or are making it up at the time of the review and are likely to give valuable hints about the exam. Other instructors indicate the probable emphasis in their exams when they distribute reviews or study guides. You should, of course, consider these aids very carefully.

5 Questions on past quizzes and reviews as well as tests at the end of textbook chapters.

If you follow these suggestions, you will have identified most of, if not all, the key concepts in the course.

GENERAL TIPS: BEFORE THE EXAM

Whether you follow a conscientious study schedule or have time only to cram at the last minute (see page 109), the following suggestions will help you make the most of your time right before the test.

1 Spend the night before an exam making a final review of your notes. Then go right to bed without watching television or otherwise interfering with the material you have learned. Your mind will tend to work through and absorb the material during the night. To further lock in your learning, get up a half hour earlier than usual the next morning and review your notes.

2 Make sure you take with you any materials (pen, paper, eraser, dictionary, and other aids allowed) you will need during the exam.

3 Be on time for the exam. If you arrive late, you are setting yourself up to do poorly.

4 Sit in a quiet spot. Some people are very talkative and noisy before an exam. Since you don't want anything to interfere with your learning, you are better off not talking with others the few minutes before the exam starts. In fact, you might want to use those minutes to make one final review of your notes.

5 Read over carefully all the directions on the exam before you begin. Many students don't take this important step and end up losing points because they fail to do what is required. Make sure you understand how you are expected to respond to each item, how many points each section is worth, and, equally important, how many questions you must answer. Also listen carefully to any verbal directions or hints the instructor may give. Many students shipwreck their chances right at the start because they do not understand or follow directions. Don't let this happen to you.

6 Budget your time. Take a few seconds to figure out roughly how much time you can spend on each section of the test. Write the number of minutes in the margin of your exam paper or on a scratch sheet. Then stick to that schedule. Be sure to have a watch with you or to sit where you can see a clock.

   Exactly *how* you budget your time depends on what kinds of questions you are good at answering (and so can do more quickly) and the point value of different sections of the test. Keep in mind that the reason for budgeting your time is to prevent you from ending up with ten minutes left and a fifty-point essay still to write or thirty multiple-choice questions to answer.

PREPARING FOR AND TAKING OBJECTIVE EXAMS

Objective exams may include multiple-choice, true-false, fill-in, and matching questions. Perhaps you feel that objective tests do not require as much study time as essay exams. A well-constructed objective test, however, can evaluate your understanding of major concepts and demand just as sophisticated a level of thinking as an essay exam. In short, do not cut short your study time just because you know you will be given an objective test.

   To do well on objective tests, you must know how to read test items carefully. The pages that follow describe a number of strategies you can use to deal with the special problems posed by objective tests.

Getting Ready for Objective Exams

1   Ask your instructor what kind of items will be on the test. Not all instructors will provide this information. However, finding out beforehand that an exam will include, let's say, fifty multiple-choice and fifty fill-in items relieves you of some anxiety. At least you know what to expect.

2   Try to find a test that is similar to the one you will be taking. Some instructors distribute past exams to help students review. Also, some departments keep on file exams given in earlier semesters. Looking at these exams closely can familiarize you with the requirements, format, and items you may reasonably expect on your exam.

3   Be sure to review carefully all the main points presented in the course. These were detailed in "What to Study" on pages 94 and 95. To sharpen your understanding of the course's key material, apply the techniques of repeated self-testing (page 85) to the recall words written in the margin of your class and textbook notes (pages 30 and 51).

4   Make up practice test items when you study. That way you will be getting into the rhythm of taking the test, and you may even be able to predict some of the questions the instructor will ask.

Taking Objective Exams

1   Answer all the easier questions first. Don't lose valuable time stalling over hard questions. You may end up running out of time and not even getting a chance to answer the questions you can do easily. Instead, put a light check mark (√) beside difficult questions and continue working through the entire test, answering all the items you can do right away. You will find that this strategy will help give you the momentum you need to go confidently through the rest of the exam.

2   Go back and spend the time remaining with the difficult questions you have marked. Often you will find that while you were answering the easier questions, your unconscious mind has been working on questions you at first found very difficult. Or later items may have provided just the extra bit of information you need to answer earlier items you found difficult. Once you answer a question, add a mark to the check you have already made (✗) to show you have completed that item.

3   Answer *all* questions, unless the instructor has said that points will be deducted for wrong answers. Guess if you must; by doing so, you are bound to pick up at least a few points.

4   Ask the instructor to explain any item that isn't clear. Not all instructors will provide this explanation but probably many will. Most experienced instructors realize that test questions may seem clear and unambiguous to them as they make up the exam but that students may interpret certain questions in other and equally valid ways. In short, you can't lose anything by asking to have an item clarified.

5   Put yourself in the instructor's shoes when you try to figure out the meaning of a confusing item. In light of what was covered in the course, which answer do you think the instructor would say is correct? If a test item is worded so ambiguously that no single response seems correct, you may—in special situations—use the margin of your test paper to explain to the instructor what you feel the answer should be. Obviously, use this technique only when absolutely necessary.

6   Circle or underline the key words in difficult questions. This strategy can help you untangle complicated questions and focus on the central point in the item.

7   Express difficult questions in your own words. Rephrasing the item in simpler terms and then writing it down or even saying it to yourself can help you cut through the confusion and get to the core of the question. Be sure, however, not to change the meaning of the original item.

8   Take advantage of the full time given and go over the exam carefully for possible mistakes. People used to say that it was not a good idea to change the first answer you put down. However, as long as you have a good reason, you *should* change your earlier answers if they seem incorrect. At the same time, be on guard against last-minute anxiety that prompts you to change, without good reason, *many* of your original answers. You should control any tendency you may have to make widespread revisions.

Specific Hints for Answering Multiple-Choice Questions
1   Remember that you may not always be given a perfect answer to every question. In such cases, you must choose the best answer available.

2   Cross out answers you know are incorrect. Eliminating answers in this way is helpful because it focuses your attention on the most

reasonable options. If you think all options are incorrect, the correct answer would be "none of the above."

3   Be sure to read all the possible answers to a question, especially when the first answer is correct. Remember that the other options could also be correct. In this case, "all of the above" would be the correct response.

4   Minimize the risk of guessing the answer to difficult items by doing either of the following:

   a. Read the question and then the first possible answer. Next, read the question again and the second possible answer and so on until you have read the question with each separate answer. Breaking the items down this way will often help you identify the option that most logically answers the question.

   b. Try not to look at the answers when you return to difficult items. Instead, read the question, supply your own answer, and then look for the option on the test which is closest to your response.

5   Be alert for the following clues which may signal *correct* answers:

   a. The longest answer is often correct. For example:

   > The key reason students who are well prepared still don't do well on exams is that they (a) are late to the test, (b) don't have all their materials, (c) forget to jot down catch phrases, (d) haven't studied enough, (e) don't read all the directions before they begin the test

   The correct answer is *e*, the longest answer.

   b. The most complete and inclusive answer is often correct. For example:

   > If you have to cram for a test, which of these items should receive most of your attention? (a) The instructor's tests from other years, (b) important ideas in the class and text notes, including such things as key terms, their definitions, and clarifying examples, (c) the textbook, (d) class notes, (e) textbook notes

   The correct answer is *b*, the most complete and inclusive choice. (Note that the most complete answer is also often the longest.)

   c. An answer in the middle, especially one with the most words, is often correct. For example:

   > Many students have trouble with objective tests because they (a) guess when they're not sure, (b) run out of time,

(c) think objective exams are easier than essay tests and so do not study enough, (d) forget to double check their answers, (e) leave difficult questions to the end.

The correct answer is *c*, the answer in the middle with the most words.

d. If two answers have the opposite meaning, one of them is probably correct. For example:

Before an exam starts, you should (a) sit in a quiet spot, (b) join a group of friends and talk about the test, (c) review the textbook one last time, (d) read a book and relax, (e) study any notes you didn't have time for previously.

The correct answer is *a*. Note that *a* and *b* are roughly opposite in meaning.

e. Answers with qualifiers such as *generally, probably, most, often, some, sometimes,* and *usually* are frequently correct. For example:

In multiple-choice questions, the most complete and inclusive answer is (a) never correct, (b) often correct, (c) always correct, (d) all of the above, (e) none of the above.

The correct answer is *b*, the choice with the qualifying word *often*.

6 Be alert for the following clues which may signal *incorrect* answers:

a. If two answers are close in meaning, both are probably incorrect. For example:

To budget your time on an exam, you should (a) do difficult questions first, (b) leave easier questions to the end, (c) leave time to review, (d) make up a schedule and stick to it, (e) save essays for last.

The correct answer is *d*. Note that *a* and *b* have the same meaning; both are incorrect.

b. Answers with absolute words such as *all, always, everyone, everybody, never, no one, nobody, none,* and *only* are usually incorrect. For example:

In multiple-choice questions, the answer in the middle with the most words is (a) always correct, (b) always incorrect, (c) frequently correct, (d) never wrong, (e) never right.

The correct answer is *c;* all the other answers use absolute words and are incorrect.

Specific Hints for Anwering True-False Questions

1 Simplify questions with double negatives by crossing out both negatives and then determining the correct answer. For example:

> T_____ F_____ You won't be unprepared for essay exams if you anticipate several questions and prepare your answers for those questions.

can reworked to read:

> T_____ F_____ You will be prepared for essay exams if you anticipate several questions and prepare your answers for those questions.

This statement is true. Here is another example:

> T_____ F_____ An objective test is not without pitfalls.

When the negatives are omitted, the question reads:

> T_____ F_____ An objective test has pitfalls.

This statement is true.

2 Remember that answers with qualifiers such as *generally, probably, most, often, some, sometimes,* and *usually* are frequently true. For example:

> T_____ F_____ Some instructors will tell students what kind of items to expect on an exam.

The statement is true.

3 Remember that answers with absolute words such as *all, always, everyone, everybody, never, no one, nobody, none,* and *only* are usually false. For example:

> T_____ F_____ You should never review your notes the morning of an essay.

The statement is false.

Specific Hints for Answering Fill-in Questions

1 Read questions to yourself so you can actually hear what is being asked. If more than one response comes to mind, write them both lightly in the margin. Then when you review your answers later, choose the answer that feels most right to you.

2 Make sure each answer you provide fits logically and grammatically into its slot in the sentence. For example:

> An _____ lists ideas in a sequence.

The correct answer is *enumeration*. Note that the word *an* signals that the correct answer begins with a vowel.

3   Remember that not all fill-in answers require only one word. If you feel that several words are needed to complete an answer, write in all the words, unless the instructor or the directions indicate that only single-word responses will be accepted.

Specific Hints for Answering Matching Questions

1   Don't start matching items until you have read both columns and gotten a sense of the alternatives. Often, there's an extra item or two in one column. This means that not all items can be paired. Some will be left over. For example:

1. Sentence skills mistakes	a. compare, explain, analyze
	_____ b. often, usually, most
2. Absolute words _____	c. from, over, in, with
3. Connecting words _____	d. misspelled and omitted words
4. Qualifying words _____	
5. Direction words in instructions	e. all, never, only
	_____ f. first, second, next, also

The correct answers are 1-d, 2-e, 3-f, 4-b, and 5-a. Item *c* is extra.

2   Start, as always, with the easiest items. One by one, focus on each item in one column and look for its match in the other column. Cross out items as you use them.

PREPARING FOR AND TAKING ESSAY EXAMS

Essay exams are perhaps the most common type of writing you will do in school. They include one or several questions to which you must respond in detail, writing your answers in a clear, well-organized manner. Many students have trouble with essay exams because they do not realize there is a sequence to follow that will help them do well on such tests. Here are five steps you should master if you want to write effective exam essays:

1. Anticipate ten probable questions.
2. Prepare and memorize an informal outline answer for each question.
3. Look at the exam carefully and do several things.
4. Prepare a brief, informal outline before answering an essay question.
5. Write a well-organized, careful essay.

The following pages offer explanations and illustrations of these steps.

Step 1 Anticipate Ten Probable Questions

Because time is limited, your instructor can ask, at most, only several questions on a test. If you have done an effective job preparing for the exam (See "What to Study," pages 94 and 95), you have already identified the most important concepts discussed in class, in the textbook, and in any other assigned reading. You are well on your way to being able to predict, with reasonable certainty, the questions that will appear on the essay exam.

Now, based on the key concepts you have identified, prepare a list of ten essay questions the instructor is likely to ask. You will find that preparing these questions will deepen your understanding of the ideas covered in the course. Also, you will have a sharper sense of the relationships among the different parts of the material.

An Illustration of Step 1

A psychology class was told to prepare for an essay exam based on material presented in a lecture and a textbook chapter. The subject under discussion was adolescent development. Carl, one student in the class, followed the suggestions presented in "What to Study" (pages 94 and 95) and was able to identify ten questions the instructor was apt to ask. Three of these questions are listed below.

- What is the difference between the traditional and the modern theory of adolescence?
- What are some of the problems adolescents have?
- How can adults make adolescence a less difficult time for teenagers?

Step 2 Prepare and Memorize an Informal Outline Answer for Each Question*

For each question, do the following:

1 Write out the question and under it list the main points that need to be discussed.

2 Put important supporting information in parentheses after each main point. You now have an informal outline.

* *Note:* If you have spelling problems, make up and memorize a list of difficult-to-spell words you will probably use in your answer. For example, for a test on adolescent development, you might study the spelling of such words as *adolescence, emotionality, ambiguity,* and *independence.*

3 Circle the key word(s) in each main point.

4 Directly below the outline, write the first letter of each key word. Write the letters one after another.

5 Use the letters you have recorded (either rearranged or in the original order) to make up an easily remembered catch phrase. The purpose of this catch phrase is to pull into memory the key words represented by the letters and so the content of the informal outline.

6 Test yourself repeatedly until you can recall the key words the letters stand for and the main points the key words represent. (*Note:* For a full explanation of and practice in memory training, see Chapter 6.)

This outlining and memorization process is illustrated below.

An Illustration of Step 2

Here is how Carl outlined and put into effect a recall system for three of the ten questions he believed might appear on the exam.

- *Question 1:* What is the difference between the traditional and the modern theory of adolescence?
  1. (Biologically generated.) Universal phenomenon (Hall's theory: hormonal)
  2. (Sociologically generated) Not universal phenomenon (not purely hormonal)

  BG SG: BIG GUY   SMALL GUY

- Question 2: What are some of the problems adolescents have?
  1. Reality of (economic dependence) conflicts with need for independence
  2. (Ambiguity) of status (too old for some things; too young for others; creates resentment and frustration)
  3. Increased (emotionality) (introspection, instability, impatience, rebelliousness, isolation)

  EDAE: ED DUCKS ALL EXAMS

- Question 3: How can adults make adolescence a less difficult time for teenagers?

  (Chapman's) Theory: The Three L's
  1. (Love) and support (personalized guidance)
  2. (Limitations) (unrestricted freedom perceived as lack of care)
  3. (Let) adolescents be

  CLLL: CAROL LIKES LICORICE LOTS

Step 3 Look at the Exam Carefully and Do Several Things

1 Get an overview of the exam by reading *all* the questions on the test.

2 Note the direction words (*compare, illustrate, list,* and so on) for each question. Be sure to write the kind of answer that each question requires. For example, if a question says "illustrate," do not "compare." The list below will help clarify the distinctions among various direction words.

Compare	Show similarities between things.
Contrast	Show differences between things.
Criticize	Give the positive and negative points of a subject as well as evidence for these positions.
Define	Give the formal meaning of a term.
Describe	Tell in detail about something.
Diagram	Give a drawing and label it.
Discuss	Give details and, if relevant, the positive and negative points of a subject as well as evidence for these positions.
Enumerate	List points and number them 1, 2, 3. . . .
Evaluate	Give the positive and negative points of a subject as well as your judgment about which outweighs the other and why.
Illustrate	Explain by giving examples.
Interpret	Explain the meaning of something.
Justify	Give reasons for something.
List	Give a series of points and number them 1, 2, 3. . . .
Outline	Give the main points and important secondary points. Put main points at the margin and indent secondary points under the main points. Relationships may also be described with logical symbols, as follows:

    1. _____
      a. _____
      b. _____
    2. _____

Prove	Show to be true by giving facts or reasons.
Relate	Show connections among things.

State	Give the main points.
Summarize	Give a condensed account of the main points.
Trace	Describe the development or history of a subject.

3 Start with the least demanding question. Getting a good answer down on paper will build your confidence and make it easier to tackle the more difficult items. Number you answers clearly so the instructor knows the order in which you are answering the questions.

An Illustration of Step 3

Two questions appeared on the essay exam given in the adolescent psychology class. Below is the first question. Note how closely it parallels and combines three of the questions Carl made up when preparing for the exam (see page 103).

> Contrast the traditional and contemporary theories which explain the strain and stress of adolescence. List several typical stressful problems adolescents face and summarize one approach adults can use to ease adolescents' transition to adulthood.

After reading the questions, Carl underlined the direction words *contrast, list,* and *summarize* to remind himself how to present his answer. Also, since Carl was especially well prepared to respond to the first question, he decided to answer it immediately and noted in the margin that he should spend only twenty-five minutes on this answer, leaving himself thrity-five minutes to respond to a second, more demanding question.

Step 4 Prepare a Brief, Informal Outline
Before Answering an Essay Question

Use the margin of the exam or a separate piece of scratch paper to jot down quickly, as they occur to you, the main points you want to discuss in each answer. Then decide in what order you want to present these points in your response. Put *1* in front of the first item, *2* beside the second, and so on. You now have an informal outline to guide you as you answer your essay question.

If there is a question on the exam which is similar to the questions you anticipated and outlined at home, quickly write down the catch phrase that calls back the content of the outline. Below the catch phrase, write the key words represented by each letter in the catch phrase. The key words, in turn, will remind you of the concepts they represent. If you have prepared properly, this step will take only a minute or so, and you will have before you the guide you need to write a focused, supported, organized answer.

An Illustration of Step 4

As soon as Carl saw the first question on the exam, he realized he could use three of the answers he had outlined at home. To make sure he didn't forget any information, he took a few seconds to write down the catch phrases, the first letter and the key words that called back material he had outlined. Here, for example, is what his notes looked like:

BIG GUY   SMALL GUY

BG   Biologically generated
SG   Sociologically generated

ED DUCKS ALL EXAMS

E   Economic
D   Dependence
A   Ambiguity
E   Emotionality

CAROL LIKES LICORICE LOTS

C   Chapman
L   Love
L   Limits
L   Let be

Step 5   Write a Well-Organized, Careful Essay

If you have followed the suggestions to this point, you have done all the preliminary work needed to write an effective essay. Be sure not to wreck your chances of getting a good grade by writing carelessly. Instead, as you prepare your response, keep in mind the principles of good writing: unity, support, organization, and clear, error-free sentences (see pages 117 to 126).

First, start your essay with one or two main-idea sentences that clearly indicate the direction of your response—for example: "There are several schools of thought in contemporary psychology"; "Although there were many consequences of the industrial revolution, these were the ones felt most sharply early in the twentieth century"; "High-rise apartment buildings contribute in several ways to many of the sociological problems associated with urban living"; "The back-to-basics movement in education can be seen as a reaction to several trends in the 1960s."

Second, although you obviously must take time limitations into account, develop your main ideas as much as possible. Instructors expect you to demonstrate your understanding of the points being made. A point that you mention quickly and never develop usually carries very little weight.

Third, use connecting words to guide your reader through your answer. For instance, words and phrases such as *the first reason, next, also, by way of contrast, however, finally* make it easy for the reader to follow your line of thought.

Fourth, unless an outline or simple list of numbered items is called for, write your answer in complete sentences.

Finally, leave time to proofread your essay for sentence skills mistakes you may have made while you concentrated on writing your answer. Look for words omitted, miswritten, or misspelled (if possible, bring a dictionary with you); for awkward phrasings or misplaced punctuation marks; for whatever else may prevent the reader from understanding your thought. Cross out any mistakes and make your corrections neatly above the errors. If you want to add to or change some point, insert an asterisk at the appropriate spot, put another asterisk at the bottom of the page, and enter the corrected or additional material there.

An Illustration of Step 5

Here is Carl's response to the essay question on page 106. Notice that he uses the material he developed in steps 1 to 4 to prepare his answer. Also, note how his response reflects a careful consideration of the guidelines just outlined in step 5. He has, in short, written a well-organized, careful essay.

CARL'S ESSAY ANSWER

> There is a significant difference between the traditional and contemporary theories explaining the turbulence of adolescence. The earlier theory, advanced by G. Stanley Hall, held that the stresses of adolescence were universal; all youngsters, because of extensive biological changes taking place in their bodies, went through troubled times as they made the transition to adulthood. By way of contrast, the current view states, first, that adolescence

is not a troubled time in all cultures, and so this period in young people's lives cannot be caused by purely hormonal changes.

Second, the modern theory holds that the stresses of adolescence are caused by the society in which a youngster lives.*

    For example, the following three issues make adolescence a difficult time for young people in this country:

1. Adolescents' economic dependence on adults. This situation presents a problem since adolescents must also work toward independence from their elders.

2. Adolescents' ambiguous status. They straddle two worlds: too big and old for some things, too small and young for others. This predicament causes tension and frustration.

3. Increased emotionality. The issues just listed lead to what is seen as the characteristic temperament of teenagers: their introspectiveness, argumentativeness, hostility, rebelliousness.

    Adolescence is indeed a troubled time in our society. However, Chapman suggests that adolescence would be a less traumatic period if adults adopted the "L" approach. They should love teenagers, establish reasonable limits for them, and just let them be.

* Consequently, the kind of pressures that adolescents face will vary from culture to culture.

A FINAL NOTE: HOW TO CRAM WHEN YOU HAVE NO OTHER CHOICE

Students who consistently cram for tests are not likely to be successful in their courses. They often have to cram because they have not managed their time well. However, even organized students may sometimes run into problems that disrupt their regular study routine. As a result, they need to cram in order to pass a test. If you're ever in this situation, the following steps may help you do some quick but effective studying.

1   Accept the fact that, in the limited time you have, you are not going to be able to study everything in your class notes and textbook. You may even have to exclude your textbook if you know that your teacher tends to base most of a test on class material.

2 Read through your class notes (and, if you have them, your textbook notes) and mark off those ideas that are most important. Use as a guide any review or study sheets that your instructor has provided. Your purpose is to try to guess correctly many of the ideas your teacher will put in the test.

  Important ideas often include definitions, enumerations (list of items), points marked by emphasis words, and answers to basic questions made out of titles and headings. See also "What to Study" on pages 94 and 95.

3 Write the ideas you have selected on sheets of paper, using one side of a page only. Perhaps you will wind up with three or four "cram sheets" full of important points to study.

4 Prepare catch words or phrases to recall the material and then memorize the points using the method of repeated self-testing described on page 85 and discussed in detail in Chapter 6.

5 Go back, if the time remains, and review all your notes. If you do not have textbook notes, you might skim your textbook. Do not use this time to learn new concepts. Instead, try to broaden as much as possible your understanding of the points you have already studied.

Activities

1 Review the chapter carefully. Then, without looking back, take the following quiz. You have five kinds of questions to answer, with these point values for each section: following directions, 10 points; matching, 30 points; fill-ins, 20 points; true-false, 20 points; and multiple choice, 20 points.

A. *Following directions.*   Print your full name, last name first, on the line at the right-hand side above. Write your full name, first name last, under the line at the left-hand side above.

B. *Matching.*   Enter the appropriate letter in the space provided next to each definition.

1. Show similarities between two things. _____
2. Explain by giving examples. _____
3. Give the formal meaning of a term. _____
4. Words that tell you exactly what to do. _____
5. Give a series of points and number them 1, 2, 3, etc. _____
6. Give a condensed account of the main points. _____

a. Define
b. Contrast
c. Direction words
d. List
e. Compare
g. Illustrate
h. Summarize

C. *Fill-ins.*   Write the word or words needed to complete each of the following sentences.

1. You should _____ consistently in order to avoid last-minute cram situations that may cause exam panic.

2. On either an objective or essay exam, you will build up confidence and momentum if you do the easier questions _____ .

3. Because essay exam time is limited, instructors can give you only several questions to answer. They will reasonably focus on questions dealing with the _____ areas of the subject.

4. Before starting an objective or essay test, you should _____ _____ your time.

D. *True or false.*   Write out the word *True* or *False* to the left of the following statements.

_____ 1. Often the main reason that students choke or block on exams is that they are not well prepared.

_____ 2. When studying for an essay test, prepare a good outline answer for each question and memorize the outlines.

_____ 3. If you have to cram, you should try to study everything in your class notes and textbook.

_____ 4. You should spend the night before an exam organizing your notes.

E. Multiple choice. Circle the letter of the answer that best completes each of the following statements.

1. One step that is *not* necessarily recommended in preparing for and taking an essay exam is to (a) list ten or so probable questions, (b) prepare an outline answer for each question, (c) focus on the details in your class and text notes, (d) understand direction words.

2. When taking an objective test, remember that (a) absolute statements are always false, (b) absolute statements are often false, (c) absolute statements are never false, (d) a and c only.

3. When taking an essay exam, you should (a) outline your answers before you begin to write, (b) be direct when you write, (c) use signal words to guide your reader through the answer, (d) all of the above, (e) none of the above.

4. In preparing for an objective or essay exam, pay attention to (a) key terms and their definitions, (b) major lists of items, (c) points emphasized in class or in the text, (d) all of the above.

2   Evaluate your present test preparation and test-taking skills. Put a check mark beside each of the following steps that you already practice. Then put a check mark beside those steps that you plan to practice. Leave a space blank if you do not plan to follow a particular point.

What to Study	Now Do	Plan to Do
1. Key terms, definitions, and examples		
2. Enumerations (lists of items)		
3. Points emphasized in class		
4. Reviews and study guides		
5. Questions in past quizzes and textbook chapters		
General Tips Before an Exam		
1. Study right before sleep.		
2. Take materials needed to the exam.		
3. Be on time for the exam.		
4. Sit in a quiet spot.		

5. Read all directions carefully.
6. Budget your time.

Getting Ready for Objective Exams
1. Ask instructor about makeup of test.
2. Look at similar tests.
3. Review carefully all main points of course.
4. Make up practice test items.

Taking Objective Exams
1. Answer all easier questions first.
2. Do difficult questions in time remaining.
3. Anwer all questions.
4. Ask instructor to explain unclear items.
5. Think of instructor's point of view with difficult questions.
6. Mark key words in difficult questions.
7. State difficult questions in own words.
8. Use all time given.
9. Use specific hints given for multiple-choice, true-false, fill-in, and matching questions.

Preparing for and Taking Essay Tests
1. List ten or so probable questions.
2. Prepare a good outline answer for each question and memorize the outline.
3. Look at the exam carefully and:
   a. Read *all* the questions.
   b. Note direction words.
   c. Start with the easiest question.
4. Outline answer before writing it.
5. Write a well-organized answer by:
   a. Having a main-idea sentence
   b. Using connecting signals throughout the answer
   c. Writing complete sentences
   d. Proofreading paper for:
      • Omitted words
      • Miswritten words
      • Unclear phrasing and punctuation
      • Misspellings

3 Answer the questions that follow by using the specific hints for multiple-choice, true-false, fill-in, and matching test items that have been presented in this chapter. In the space provided, indicate the hint used to determine the correct answer.

Multiple-Choice Items

1. The first step in preparing for an essay exam is to (a) read the questions carefully, (b) study with other students, (c) anticipate several questions you may reasonably expect on the test, (d) review the textbook, (e) none of the above.

   Correct answer _____   Hint used (see pages 98 to 100)

   _____

2. Difficult questions should (a) be done before easier items, (b) be done after easier items, (c) never be guessed at, (d) all of the above, (e) none of the above.

   Correct answer _____   Hint used (see pages 98 to 100)

   _____

3. Being prepared for exams means you (a) go to class regularly, (b) read assigned material, (c) take class and textbook notes, (d) memorize your notes, (e) all of the above.

   Correct answer _____   Hint used (see pages 98 to 100)

   _____

True-False Items

4. T_____ F_____ Everybody finds essay exams more demanding than objective exams.

   Correct answer _____   Hint used (see page 101)

   _____

5. T_____ F_____ It is not true that teachers are incapable of making up unclear tests.

   Correct answer _____   Hint used (see page 101)

   _____

6. T_____ F_____ You should usually try to express a difficult or confusing question in your own words.

   Correct answer _____   Hint used (see page 101)

   _____

4 Spend a half hour getting ready to write a one-paragraph essay on the question: "Describe eight points to remember when planning a weekly study schedule." The eight points are described on pages 13 to 16. When the half hour is up, put your notes away and write your essay answer.

5 Prepare five questions you might be expected to answer on an essay exam in one of your courses. Make up an outline answer for each of the five questions. Memorize one of the outlines, using the technique of repeated self-testing (see pages 85 to 88). Finally, write a full essay answer, in complete sentences, to one of the questions. Your instructor may ask you to hand in your five outlines and the essay.

6 Read the following description of one student's study situation:

> Most of the exams Rita takes include both multiple-choice and true-false questions as well as at least one essay question. She has several problems with such tests. She often goes into the test in a state of panic. "As soon as I see a question I can't answer," she says, "big chunks of what I do know just fly out the window. I go into an exam expecting to choke and forget." Another problem is her timing. "Sometimes I spend too much time trying to figure out the answer to tricky multiple-choice or true-false questions. Then I end up with only fifteen minutes to answer two essay questions." Rita's greatest difficulty is writing essay answers. "Essays are where I always lose a lot of points. Sometimes I don't read a question the right way, and I wind up giving the wrong answer to the question. When I do understand a question, I have trouble organizing my answer. I'll be halfway through an answer and then realize that I skipped some material I should have put at the start, or that I already wrote down something I should have saved for the end. I have a friend who says that essays are easier to study for because she can usually guess what the questions will be. I don't see how this is possible. Essay tests really scare me since I never know what questions are coming."

Write a one-page (or longer) essay in which you answer in detail the question: "What specific steps can Rita take to overcome her problems with tests?" Apply the information you have learned in Chapter 7.

8

Writing Effective Papers

This chapter will show you how to:

- Achieve the standards of effective writing in your work

- Prepare your paper in a series of stages

STEPS IN WRITING EFFECTIVELY

One way that instructors can see if you understand course material is by having you write about ideas presented in the course. Perhaps, however, you are one of those many students who panic when asked to put ideas down on paper. Whether a one-paragraph exam essay or a fifteen-page research paper is involved, you may feel that writing effectively is beyond you. Writing may seem like something that people with a special gift can do, but for which you lack the necessary talent.

To overcome this attitude, you need to realize that the principles of effective writing are not mysterious and complex. In fact, writing is a skill, like swimming, cooking, or typing. As with any skill, you can learn to write with confidence once you understand and master certain basic ground rules. "And so," you are probably wondering, "what are the essentials? What are the basic steps I really need to know to write an effective paper?" To write effectively, follow these four steps:

1. State a central point at the beginning of the paper.
2. Provide specific evidence to support that point.
3. Organize the support in a logical, easy-to-follow way.
4. Write clear, error-free sentences.

If you follow all four steps, your papers will be *unified, supported, organized,* and *error-free.* These qualities, in turn, are the essential features of effective writing. This section of the chapter explains each of the four steps.

STEP 1 MAKING AND STICKING TO A POINT

Your first step in writing is to decide what point you want to make. Decide, in other words, what central idea, assertion, or statement you want to advance. As a guide to yourself and the reader, express that point in one or more sentences near the beginning of the paper. You may, in fact, express the main idea in the *first* sentence. Then, if you are sure that everything else in your paper is directly related to and develops this main idea, you will have written a *unified* paper.

Two Paragraphs to Consider

The two paragraphs that follow were written by two different students in answer to this essay question on a psychology exam: "Explain and illustrate briefly three defense mechanisms used by many people."

You will see that one paragraph does not start with a clear opening point. Not surprisingly, the writer of that paragraph went off in several directions rather than consistently developing a single point; the other student's answer was sharply focused throughout. Read both paragraphs carefully, and note which one loses sight of the opening point.

Three of the most commonly used defense mechanisms are rationalization, compensation, and repression. When we rationalize or "make excuses," we keep from ourselves the real motive for our behavior and give a different motive instead. For instance, some students may be too lazy to study for a test. But instead of admitting this, they'll tell themselves that it's too late to study or they're too busy to study. Another defense mechanism is compensation, which means that we make up for some ability we don't have by substituting one we do possess. For example, an unathletic boy who can't be a success in outdoor sports may redirect his energies so he becomes a success in a mental sport like chess. A final defense mechanism is repression, in which we "push down" to an unconscious level experiences that cause anxiety. Thus, we might actually forget that we owe a certain bill if there is not enough money in our checking account to cover it. These are only three of a number of defense mechanisms people use in daily life.

Freud was the first one to describe the way defense mechanisms help us control anxiety and keep up our self-esteem. People use defense mechanisms frequently in their everyday lives. In rationalization, we "make excuses" and don't admit to ourselves the real reasons for our behavior. Of all the defense mechanisms, rationalization is one that everyone practices quite often. It allows us to feel better about ourselves than we would otherwise. Freud spent a lot of time helping patients uncover the rationalizations that created conflict in their lives. Another defense mechanism is compensation. Life is full of compensations in which we get satisfactions that we might not otherwise obtain. A person who isn't a social success might try to be an academic success instead. This, however, is a situation where a defense mechanism may be carried to extremes. People may completely cut themselves off socially when in fact they should be learning how to deal with their shyness. Mature individuals are ones who at times use defense mechanisms, yet keep them from becoming obsessive or distorting reality.

Fill in the missing words: The _____ paragraph is effective for it consistently develops one point. The _____ paragraph is not unified because it includes details and ideas not related to the opening point.

The first paragraph is more effective because it is *unified.* All the details in the paragraph develop the main point; they provide explanations and examples of three different defense mechanisms. In contrast, the second paragraph has no opening statement and so it is not apparent why certain information (the details about Freud, the frequency of rationalization, the dangers of compensation) has been included. Without the clear statement of a single opening point, the paragraph ends up going in several directions. The paragraph is unfocused and, in short, lacks unity.

Summary of Step 1

Whether you are writing an exam essay or a paper, remember that your first aim should be to make a point and stick to that point. In other words, the first standard of effective writing is unity. You achieve unity in a paper when the details support and develop the main idea expressed at the start of the paper. Each time you think of something to put into your paper, ask yourself whether it relates to your main point. If it does not, leave it out. For example, if you wrote a paper explaining why school can be a frightening experience for small children and then spent a paragraph or two talking about how schools help children, your paper would not be unified. You would be missing the first and most essential principle of effective writing.

STEP 2   SUPPORTING A CENTRAL POINT WITH SPECIFIC EVIDENCE

The second essential step in writing effectively is to support with specific evidence the central point you want to make in the paper. The evidence that supports and develops a point is made up of specific facts, definitions, reasons, details, examples, and so on. Note how the definitions and examples in the unified answer on defense mechanism support the main point of the paragraph.

Two Paragraphs to Consider

The paragraphs that follow were written in response to this question on a history exam: "Summarize the five key factors that led to the Great Depression." Both paragraphs begin by clearly stating the point of the essay. But as you read each paragraph, you will see that only one answer provides sufficient specific evidence to support the central point.

Five key factors led to the Great Depression of 1929 to 1933. One cause was rapid technological progress. This meant that many workers were unemployed. Another cause was an unequal distribution of income. People at the subsistence level had no money to spend on goods. Two more factors were the abuses of large corporations as well as abuses in the stock market. A final cause was the lack of action on the part of the federal government to remedy some of the problems in the economy.

Five key factors led to the Great Depression of 1929 to 1933. One cause was that the rapid technological progress of the 1920s led to the loss of a number of jobs. In farming and in the textile and coal industries, people were replaced by machines. By the end of the 1920s, one out of seven people was unemployed. A second cause of the Depression was the unequal distribution of national income. For example, because so many people were unemployed by 1929, only 1 percent of the population could afford to buy consumer products. This meant there was a limited market for the increasing number of goods being produced. The resulting upset in the supply and demand balance led to the third cause of the Depression: the pricing policies of the great corporations. Since there was no competition for goods, corporations set unrealistically high prices and so contributed to the growing imbalance between consumption and production. A fourth factor in the Depression was excessive stock market speculation. People invested money in the market even after stock prices became inflated. Money that could have been put into new industries, and that would have created new jobs, was put instead into nonproductive speculation. Finally, the federal government's lack of action contributed to the Depression. The government did not act to offset inequities in income, to correct corporation's pricing policies, or to control reckless stock market speculation. For example, the government did not brake the stock market boom by raising the down payment required for stock purchases. All these factors set the groundwork for the country's most severe economic crisis.

Fill in the missing word: The _____ paragraph provides detailed reasons to support fully the opening point.

The first writer briefly cites five factors that led to the Depression but does not supply enough supporting details to explain those factors and so solidly support the opening point. For example, the student says that two causes of the Depression were "the abuses of large corporations as well as abuses in the stock market" but doesn't even begin to explain what those abuses were. In contrast, the writer of the second paragraph provides two sentences or so of important information about each of the five factors. In short, the second paragraph is fully *supported* and thus more effective. It contains sufficient specific evidence to demonstrate the writer's understanding of the points being made.

Summary of Step 2

Whether you write an exam essay or a paper, be sure to provide sufficient specific evidence to support the central point you make. Without that evidence, you cannot demonstrate your understanding of the material, nor can you convince your reader that your point is valid. In short, your papers will meet the second standard of effective writing if they are supported.

STEP 3 ORGANIZING THE SPECIFIC EVIDENCE

Making a point and gathering the specific evidence needed to support that point are the first two steps in writing a good paper. The third step is to organize and connect the specific evidence in a clear and logical way. There are three key techniques for tying together the material in a paper: *a clear plan of organization, connecting words,* and *linking sentences.* Each technique is described briefly below.

Plan of Organization

Probably the most common way to organize material is by presenting a list of items. You may give a series of facts, definitions, reasons, details, examples, and so on. The listing method was used in the effective paragraphs you have read so far. In the first paragraph supporting material was presented as a list of defense mechanisms, and in the second paragraph as a list of the main causes of the Depression.

Connecting Words

As you move from one supporting item in a list to another, it often helps to use connecting words. Words such as *first, second, third, another, also, next, in addition, moreover,* and *finally* are called **addition signals** because they indicate to the reader that you are providing additional support for your point. Other connecting words that help clarify your ideas include **illustration signals** (*for example, for instance, specifically*), **change-of-direction signals** (*but, however, yet, in contrast, otherwise, on the other hand, on the contrary, still*), and conclusion signals (*to conclude, in short, last of all*).

Linking Sentences

A final way to show relationships among the parts of a paper is to use linking sentences. Such sentences introduce new ideas while also referring back to points already made. For example, in the effective paragraph on the Depression, note the sentence about midway through the paragraph. That sentence introduces the third cause of the Depression (the corporations' pricing policies) but also links back to the second cause (the upset in the supply and demand balance.)

Two Paragraphs to Consider

The next two paragraphs show possible responses to the following question on a sociology exam: "Describe briefly the values and drawbacks of the adolescent peer group in the socialization process." Both writers begin with a central point and support that point with the same specific details. However, as you read the paragraphs, you will note that one writer clearly organizes and connects the supporting information and the other writer does not.

The peer group has a positive and a negative effect on teenagers' socialization. First, the peer group performs a valuable function by giving teenagers a sense of security and belonging—feelings that are especially important since most adolescents feel emotionally separated from their parents. This close-knit quality of the peer group provides a second benefit to the adolescent: a shield against painful isolation. A third value of the group is that it gives teenagers a sense of personal worth. Though adults may criticize the way their children behave, teenagers still have positive feelings about themselves because they are accepted by their peers. A fourth and final advantage of the peer group is that it teaches adolescents the social skills needed to keep the group intact. All these advantages, however, can be offset by the negative influences of the peer group on teenagers' socialization. For example, the sense of belonging to the group can encourage conformity. Teenagers may give themselves over to the group's standards and abandon their ability to make independent decisions. Also, the group's togetherness may cause teenagers to become antisocial and neglect school and family responsibilities. Similarly, the sense of personal worth within the group can easily turn into snobbishness and discrimination against people not in the group. Last, because the need to connect with others is so satisfied by the group, teenagers may stop connecting with their families. In short, the values of the peer group can also be seen as having a negative side.

The peer group has a positive and a negative effect on teenagers' socialization. The peer group gives teenagers a sense of security and belonging, feelings that are especially important since most adolescents feel emotionally separated from their parents. Because teenagers enjoy getting together with their friends, they find ways to keep busy as a group and so avoid painful isolation. Teenagers may become antisocial and neglect school and family responsibilities. They may give themselves over to the group's standards and their freedom of decision may be stifled. The peer group gives teenagers a sense of personal worth. Adults may criticize the way their children behave, but teenagers still have positive feelings about themselves since they are accepted by their peers. The sense of personal worth within the group can easily turn into snobbishness and discrimination against people not in the group. The peer group teaches adolescents the social skills needed to keep the group intact. Because the need to connect with others is so satisfied by the group, teenagers may stop connecting with their families.

Fill in the missing word: The _____ paragraph organizes and connects the supporting evidence for its central point.

The first paragraph is more effective because it is *organized.* It has a clear method of organization and uses connecting words and linking sentences. The writer uses a *clear method of organization,* in this case a listing pattern, to show the four positive and negative effects of the adolescent peer group. Also note the way most of the positive influences are indicated by *connecting words* ("First, the peer group performs a valuable function . . . ," "a second benefit . . . ," "A third value . . . ," and "A fourth and final advantage . . ."). In the same way, negative effects are signaled by "For example," "Also," "Similarly," and "Last." Finally, *linking sentences* (such as "This close-knit quality of the peer group provides a second benefit to the adolescent: a shield against painful isolation") refer back to points already made and also introduce new ideas. In short, because the first paragraph uses various techniques to tie together the points being made, it emerges as a solidly organized piece of writing.

By way of contrast, the second paragraph is disjointed and confused. First, it lacks a consistent method of organization. Values and drawbacks are described in a random order rather than a logical sequence. Also, the paragraph uses almost no connecting words and has no linking sentences. For these reasons, the paragraph, even though unified and supported, is almost impossible to follow.

Summary of Step 3

The difference between these two paragraphs dramatizes the third standard of effective writing: organization. If you want to write a coherent, easy-to-follow paper, your supporting ideas and sentences must tie together. Make sure your paper has a clear plan of organization, connecting words, and linking sentences.

STEP 4 WRITING CLEAR, ERROR-FREE SENTENCES

The fourth step in writing an effective paper is to follow the agreed-upon rules or conventions of written communication. These conventions include such things as spelling, writing in complete sentences rather than in fragments, and using capital letters and punctuation marks where needed. Many students sabotage their chances of doing well in written work because they do not take the time to double-check their papers for errors in grammar, spelling, and punctuation. Because teachers often view such errors as evidence of careless thinking, you must force yourself to proofread your work closely.

Two Paragraphs to Consider

The following paragraphs were written in response to this question on a biology exam: "Describe cases in which the unplanned introduction of an animal or plant to a given region has had harmful results." Both answers are unified, supported, and organized, but you will note that one version communicates more clearly and effectively because it is free of spelling, punctuation, and grammar mistakes. The other paragraph, however, is marred by such errors and so does not communicate clearly.

> Their are many cases in which the unplanned introduction of an organism to a new region has had damaging results, for instance, starlings were brought to the U.S. in the last centuy. Because they seemed like an attractive bird, however, they turned out to present real problems. First introduced in New York City the bird has since made itself a serious pest across the country. The bird dropings deface buildings and can kill much-needed city trees, in agrikultural areas the birds consume and contaminate food intended for damestic animals. In other area, they compete seriously with hole-nesting birds. Such as the acorn woodpecker in california. Another example of the damage caused by the introduction of a new speces occured when a cactus called prickly par was taken to Australia, the cactus soon became an enormous pest. Growing in huge strands covering millions of acres. Preventing cattle from grazing or using the land. Finally, another serious mistake was made when an african strain of honeybees in the mid 1950s was brought to brazil the bees produced a great deal of honey, but they are also aggressive and a danger. Fifty stings can kill a person they chase victims ten times further then ordinery bees. To date the bees have now spread throught South america and are accepted to reach the US in the next ten to 20 years. All these examples show that before an organism is placed in a new region. Much should be known about the total ekology of the situation otherwise serous problems may result.

There are many cases in which the unplanned introduction of an organism to a new region has had damaging results. For instance, starlings were brought to the U.S. in the last century because they seemed like an attractive bird. However, they turned out to present real problems. First introduced in New York City, the bird has since made itself a serious pest across the country. The bird's droppings deface buildings and can kill much-needed city trees. In agricultural areas, the bird consumes and contaminates food intended for domestic animals; in other areas, it competes seriously with hole-nesting birds, such as the acorn woodpecker in California. Another example of the damage caused by the introduction of a new species occurred when a cactus called prickly pear was taken to Australia. The cactus soon became an enormous pest. It grew in huge strands covering millions of acres and prevented cattle from grazing or using the land. Finally, another serious mistake was made when an African strain of honeybees was brought to Brazil in the mid-1950s. The bees produce a great deal of honey, but they are also aggressive and dangerous. Fifty stings can kill a person, and the bees chase victims ten times further than ordinary bees. The bees have now spread throughout South America and are expected to reach the U.S. in the next 10 to 20 years. All these examples show that before an organism is placed in a new region, much should be known about the total ecology of the situation; otherwise, serious problems may result.

Fill in the missing word: The _____ paragraph makes its point more effectively because it follows the conventions of written communication.

The second paragraph is the one that properly applies the agreed-upon rules of competent writing. Its sentences are *clear* and *error-free*. Take a few minutes to see if you can find and correct the mistakes in the first paragraph. Comparing the first paragraph with the correct version will help you locate the errors.

Summary of Step 4

Remember, you may prepare a unified, supported, and organized paper and still be penalized for having skills errors that make your ideas hard to understand. You must, then, develop the habit of proofreading your papers. Many people resist this final step because once they get the last word down on the page, they are reluctant to do any further work. However, if you are commited to writing effective papers, you must take this last step. The following suggestions will help you check what you have written:

1 Use the time left over after an exam to proofread your essay answers carefully. With papers you write at home, try to let some time

lapse before you check the paper for skills errors. This distance will give you a more objective view of your paper, so you can detect errors with greater ease.

2 Read your paper out loud at least once. You are likely to pick up such problems as omitted words, awkward phrasings, and incomplete sentences—errors you might not detect if you only proofread the paper silently.

3 Use a dictionary to check the spelling of any words you are not sure about.

4 Have a grammar skills handbook to refer to when you are in doubt about a particular skill.

A SUMMARY OF THE FOUR STANDARDS OF EFFECTIVE WRITING

If you follow all four steps described in this chapter, your papers will be *unified, supported, organized,* and *error-free.*

Use the questions below as a guide when you write a paper. If you can answer yes to all the questions, you will have an effective piece of writing.

1 UNITY
   • Is there a clear opening statement of the central point of the paper?
   • Does all the material support and develop the opening point?

2 SUPPORT
   • Is there *specific* evidence to support the main point?
   • Is there *enough* specific evidence?

3 ORGANIZATION
   • Is the material organized in some logical, easy-to-follow way?
   • Are connecting words used to help tie together the material?
   • Are linking sentences used to show the relationship among parts of the paper?

4 ERROR-FREE SENTENCES
   • Has the paper been proofread carefully for errors in grammar, punctuation, and spelling?

STAGES IN THE WRITING PROCESS

In addition to the four standards of effective writing, there is another issue to consider if you want to turn out good papers. You should keep in mind that writing an effective paper is almost never done in one sitting. (For many people, just knowing this fact makes the prospect of writing a paper less overwhelming.) Writing is best viewed as a *process* involving a series of related stages. To prepare a paper that reflects the four standards of effective writing, you should go through the following stages in the writing process:

1. Understand and leave enough time for the assignment.
2. Focus on a specific topic.
3. Decide on a central point, prepare an outline, and gather material.
4. Write the early drafts of the paper.
5. Polish the paper.
6. Prepare the final draft of the paper.

The rest of the chapter briefly explains these stages.

STAGE 1 UNDERSTAND AND LEAVE ENOUGH TIME FOR THE ASSIGNMENT

As soon as a paper is assigned, write down when it's due on your monthly calendar (see page 12). Then be sure to schedule enough time so you get the paper done by that date.

Many teachers assign papers in class. Write down everything an instructor says about the requirements for a paper: how long it should be, whether you should use library resources, if you should include your personal reaction in the paper, and so on. If you are not certain about some part of an assignment, be sure to ask your teacher to clarify it.

Some instructors note in the course syllabus when papers are due and may not remind students about these assignments. Remember it is your responsibility to see that these papers are handed in on time.

STAGE 2 FOCUS ON A SPECIFIC TOPIC

Some instructors assign the general areas and even the specific topics students should discuss in their papers. Other instructors leave such decisions to their students. In the latter case, select an area that interests you and, if possible, one that you know something about. Narrow the general area down to a specific topic. Look at pages 164 and 165 to see how several students limited the topics of their papers. If you do not practice this narrowing process, you are apt to take on a subject that is too broad for you to discuss adequately.

The two techniques described below can help you get started in your writing as well as help you narrow a general area down to a specific topic.

Brainstorming a List

List quickly all the points or ideas you can think of about the general area you will discuss. List your thoughts in phrases or single words, one under the other. Get down everything that comes to your mind, even if an idea seems insignificant or repetitive. Don't stop and try to organize your ideas; just write them down as they come to you. Your aim when you brainstorm is to free your mind so you can accumulate as much raw material as possible—without having to put it into order or judge its value.

If you get stuck and you cannot generate a substantial list of items, ask yourself questions (*What? Who? Why? When? Where? How?*) about the general subject and the points you have already listed. You'll be surprised how your answers to these questions make additional points spring to mind.

After you finish brainstorming, look at your list and see which points seem particularly interesting or important. Those points will often help you focus on a specific topic for your paper.

Freewriting

In freewriting, you write without stopping, for ten or so minutes, about the general area of your paper. Write your thoughts as sentences, one after the other. Try to get down everything that occurs to you. Do not worry about spelling, punctuation, erasing mistakes, finding exact words, or organizing your thoughts. If you get stuck, keep writing the last word or phrase on the paper until a new idea breaks loose. Then write that down and continue as before.

In freewriting, you are not concerned with writing logically and correctly. Instead, you concentrate on transferring the flow of thoughts in your mind to the paper in front of you. After a while, you will have recorded a good deal of raw material. Look at what you write and see which ideas seem particularly interesting or important. Those ideas will often point to the specific topic of your paper.

STAGE 3   DECIDE ON A CENTRAL POINT, PREPARE AN OUTLINE, AND GATHER MATERIAL

After identifying the specific topic of your paper, you need to guide your writing. To do that, express the central point of your paper in one or more sentences. Then list briefly, in an informal outline, what you think will be the key supporting ideas to develop the central point. These supporting ideas will become the major sections of the paper. The informal outline, which will probably change as the paper progresses, serves to focus your work. It keeps you thinking about what you should and should not include in your paper. (See page 165 for an example of a preliminary or working outline.)

The kind of material you gather to support your central point depends on the kind of paper you are writing. For example, you may use library resources, your class textbook, and/or your own thoughts and experiences.

STAGE 4 WRITE THE EARLY DRAFTS OF THE PAPER

Do not feel that you have to get everything just right when you work on the first drafts of a paper. Instead, aim to get down in a reasonably organized way the supporting material for the central point of your paper. (In a paper of one paragraph, the central point is called a *topic sentence*. In a paper of more than one paragraph, the central point is called a *thesis statement*.) At this time, do not worry about smooth phrasing, spelling, punctuation, grammar, and links between paragraphs. Get down whatever you can, however you can, and move on. You will polish your writing in the next stage.

If you are writing a several-paragraph paper, you probably should prepare an introductory and a concluding paragraph. Both types of paragraphs are described below.

Introduction

The introduction should be interesting enough to attract the reader's attention. Be sure to state the paper's thesis clearly in the introduction. The thesis statement may be followed by a sentence or two indicating the paper's plan of development—the order in which major points will be discussed in the paper. For an example of an introductory paragraph that ends with a plan of development, see the final sentence of the introduction to the research paper (page 179).

The following techniques will help you write effective introductions.

1 Begin with one or more background statements about the general subject you will discuss. Then focus on the specific topic and thesis of your paper.

2 Cite some interesting or surprising facts about your topic. Then state your thesis.

3 Ask a series of interesting questions about your topic. The questions should not require simple yes or no answers and they should lead logically into the paper's thesis.

4 Relate an incident or brief story. Be sure the anecdote is relevant, flows smoothly into the rest of your introduction, and is related to your thesis.

5 Start with an interesting, significant quotation which leads smoothly into the rest of the introduction and the paper's thesis.

Conclusion

You also want to write an effective conclusion for your paper. In a short paper, you may need only a concluding sentence rather than an entire concluding paragraph. In either case, a conclusion should indicate clearly that the paper is coming to a close and lead easily from the body of the paper.

In the conclusion, you may do several things: restate the thesis of the paper, summarize the key ideas discussed, or move beyond the points made in the paper. For example, in the conclusion, you may discuss briefly the implications of the material you have covered or relate that material to an issue of broader concern or greater significance.

As you work on the drafts, keep in mind the standards of unity, support, and organization. Pay particular attention to the first two standards. Keep focusing on your central point or thesis; make sure all the paragraphs support the thesis.

STAGE 5 POLISH THE PAPER

Read everything you have written. Be as critical as you can; you want your paper to reflect the four standards of effective writing. Make certain you have clearly communicated the paper's central point. Perhaps you will want to add more evidence to support the thesis of your paper. At the same time, you may decide to eliminate material that you now realize does not really develop your thesis. Think about rearranging sections of the paper in order to achieve as clear a plan of organization as possible. Consider adding connecting words or linking sentences to tie together parts of the paper. Rework awkward sentences and check carefully for spelling, punctuation, and grammar errors. In short, do all the rewriting needed to ensure that your paper meets the four standards of effective writing: *unity, support, organization,* and *clear, error-free sentences.*

STAGE 6   PREPARE THE FINAL DRAFT OF YOUR PAPER

Now you are ready to type the paper. Follow any special guidelines distributed by your instructor. Type neatly, leave good margins, and number the pages. Prepare a title page indicating the following: the title of the paper, your name, the name of the instructor, the title of the course, and the date.

Activities

1 Review the chapter carefully. Then, without looking back, answer the following questions.

1. The first step in effective writing is to decide what _____ _____ you want to make.

2. The kind of material you gather to support the central idea in a paper may come from:
   a. Library resources   c. Your own thoughts and experiences
   b. Class textbook   d. All of the above

3. The second essential step in writing effectively is to _____ _____ with specific evidence the point you want to make in a paper.

4. True or false: _____ When you brainstorm, you list quickly all the points you can think of about your general topic.

5. Writing is best viewed as a _____ that involves a number of related stages.

6. In a paragraph, the main point is expressed in a topic sentence; in a paper with several paragraphs, the main point is expressed in a _____ .

7. Which one of the following is *not* a technique for organizing and connecting the specific evidence in a paper?
   a. Clear plan of organization   c. Connecting signals
   b. Clear, error-free sentences   d. Linking sentences

8. To guide you in your writing, you should make a preliminary _____ of your paper.

9. You must be sure to _____ the general area of a paper down to a specific topic; otherwise, the subject of your paper will be too broad.

10. True or false: _____ Connecting words such as *first, second, next,* and *also* are called addition signals.

2 Read the following description of one student's study situation:

Paula never does well on written work. She gets nervous every time an instructor gives a written assignment because she has no idea what makes up an effective paper. Recently, she worked through a brief guide on grammar and punctuation, thinking that perhaps she was losing points because her sentence skills were not solid enough. But even though her sentence skills are now strong, she still continues to get low grades on papers. Paula also consulted a composition handbook, hoping it would give her the help she needed. After reading several chapters, however, Paula was more confused than ever. There were so many rules and suggestions to follow that she couldn't possibly remember all of them. Understandably, Paula has almost given up, convinced that she will never be an effective writer.

Now write a one-page (or longer) essay in which you answer in detail the question "What essentials does Paula need to know so she can learn to write effective papers?" In your answer, apply the information presented in this chapter.

Remember to state the central point of your answer at the beginning of your paper and to develop that main point with specific details. Also, use connecting words to tie together the supporting evidence in your paper and proofread your paper carefully for sentence-skill mistakes you may have made while writing your answer. If you follow these guidelines, you will write a paper that is unified, supported, organized, and error-free.

3 In a one-page (or longer) essay, discuss some of the ways that students can become more skillful when taking tests. In your answer, apply information from Chapter 7 on taking tests. When writing your paper, go through the stages in the writing process described on pages 126 to 131. And be sure to follow the guidelines given in Activity 2 above (and on pages 117 to 126) so that you write a paper which is unified, supported, organized, and error-free.

4 In a one-page (or longer) essay, describe how students can improve their note-taking skills in class. In your answer, apply information from Chapter 3 on taking classroom notes. When writing your paper, go through the stages in the writing process described on pages 126 to 131. And be sure to follow the guidelines given in Activity 2 above (and on pages 117 to 126) so that you write a paper which is unified, supported, organized, and error-free.

5 In a one-page (or longer) essay, discuss the various ways that you or someone you know avoids doing college work. Explain how you or the other person could deal with these avoidance tactics. In your answer, apply information from Chapter 1 on doing well in college. When writing your paper, go through the stages in the writing process described on pages 126 to 131. And be sure to follow the guidelines given in Activity 2 above (and on pages 117 to 126) so that you write a paper which is unified, supported, organized, and error-free.

9

Doing a Summary

This chapter will show you how to:

• **Summarize books, articles, and other material**

• **Follow a series of steps when writing a summary**

At some point in a course, your instructor may ask you to write a summary of a book, article, TV show, etc. In a *summary* (also referred to as a *précis* or *abstract*), you reduce material in an original work to its main points and key supporting details. Unlike an outline, however, a summary does not use symbols such as I, A, 1, 2, to indicate the relation among parts of the original material.

A summary may be a word, a phrase, several sentences, or one or more paragraphs in length. The length of the summary you prepare will depend on your instructor's expectations and the length of the original work. Most often you will be asked to write a summary of one or more paragraphs.*

Writing a summary brings together a number of important reading, study, and writing skills. To condense the original matter, you must preview, read, evaluate, organize, and perhaps outline the assigned material. Summarizing, then, can be a real aid to understanding; you must "get inside" the material and realize fully what is being said before you can reduce its meaning to a few words.

HOW TO WRITE A SUMMARY

To write a summary, follow the steps described below. These steps assume that the assigned material is a book or article. However, if the original work is a TV show or film, adapt the suggestions accordingly.

1 **Take a few minutes to preview the work.**   The boxes on the next two pages explain how to preview a book and article.

2 **Read the book or article for all you can understand the first time through.**   Don't slow down or turn back. Check or otherwise mark main points and key supporting details. Pay special attention to all the items noted in the preview. Also, look for definitions, examples, and enumerations (lists of items) since these often indicate key ideas (see pages 65 to 67). You can also identify important points by turning any heads into questions and reading to find the answers to the questions (see pages 67 to 69).

3 **Go back and reread more carefully the areas you have identified as most important.**   Also, focus on other key points you may have missed in your first reading.

---

* *Note:* There is another point to consider when you write a summary. Should you prepare an *informative summary* (a completely objective, factual condensation) or an *evaluative summary* (a condensation of the work combined with your subjective reaction to the material)? In the latter case, you evaluate such things as the author's or director's style, the importance of the points made, the organization of the material, and so on. See page 142 for more information on these two kinds of summaries.

4 **Take notes on the material** (see pages 53 and 54). Concentrate on getting down the main ideas and the key supporting points.

5 **Prepare the first draft of your summary, keeping these points in mind:**

a. At the start of the summary identify the title and author of the work. With a book, include in parentheses the place of publication, publisher, and publication date. For example. "In the book *Shyness* (Reading, Massachusetts: Addison-Wesley, 1977), Philip Zimbardo discusses. . . ." With a magazine, include in parentheses the name of the magazine and the date of publication. For example: "In an article titled 'Choosing Federal Judges on Their Merits' (*Newsweek*, February 12, 1979), Melinda Beck states. . . ."

b. Don't write an overly detailed summary. Remember, the purpose of a summary is to reduce the original work to its main points and essential supporting details.

c. Express the main points and key supporting details in your own words. Do not imitate or stay too close to the style of the original work.

d. Quote from the material only to illustrate key points. To incorporate quoted material into the summary smoothly and correctly, follow the suggestions given on page 172.

HOW TO PREVIEW A BOOK

You can preview or survey a book by taking a quick look at the following:

1 **Title** The title is often the shortest possible summary of what a book is about. Think about the title for a minute and how it may summarize the whole meaning of the work.

2 **Table of contents** The contents will tell you the number of chapters in the book and the subject of each chapter. Use the contents to get a general sense of how the book is organized.

3 **Preface** Here you'll probably find why the author wrote the book. Also, the preface may summarize the main ideas developed in the book and may describe briefly how the book is organized.

4 **First and last chapters** In these chapters, the author may preview or review important ideas and themes developed in the book.

5 **Other items** Note the way the author has used headings and subheadings to organize information in the book. Check the opening and closing paragraphs of each chapter to see if they contain introductions or summaries. Look quickly at charts, diagrams, and pictures in the book since they are probably there to illustrate key points. Note any special features (index, glossary, appendixes) that may appear at the end of the book.

HOW TO PREVIEW AN ARTICLE

You can preview an article in a magazine by taking a quick look at the following:

1 **Title** Even more than with a book, the title often summarizes what the article is about. Think about the title for a minute and how it may condense the meaning of the article.

2 **Subtitle** A subtitle, if given, is a short summary appearing under or next to the title. For example, in a *Psychology Today* article entitled "Superkids," the following caption appeared: "No one knows why some children who grow up under horrendous conditions—in homes with abusive, psychotic, or desperately poor parents—seem to develop into extraordinarily competent human beings." In short, the subtitle, caption, or any other words in large print under or next to the title often provide a quick insight into the meaning of an article.

3 **First and last several paragraphs** In the first several paragraphs, the author may introduce you to the subject and state the purpose of the article. In the last several paragraphs, the writer may present conclusions or a summary. These previews or summaries can give you a quick overview of what the entire article is about.

4 **Other items** Note any heads or subheads that appear in the article. They often provide clues to the article's main points and give an immediate sense of what each section is about. Look carefully at any pictures, charts, or diagrams that accompany the article. Page space in a magazine or journal is limited, and such visual aids are generally used only when they help illustrate important points in the article. Note any words or phrases set off in *italic* or **boldface** type; such words have probably been emphasized because they deal with important points in the article.

e. Preserve the balance and proportion of the original work. If the original spent forty pages on one area and only three pages on another, your summary should reflect that emphasis.

f. Revise the first draft, paying attention to the principles of effective writing (*unity, support, organization,* and *clear, error-free sentences*) explained on pages 117 to 126.

g. Write the final draft of the paper.

A MODEL SUMMARY

Here is a model summary of a magazine article.

In an article titled "On Magic in Medicine" (*Human Nature,* January 1979), Lewis Thomas describes the widespread tendency to create easy and simplistic explanations for our most serious diseases. In the past, for example, many people believed tuberculosis was caused by night air and insufficient sunlight. This untested theory remained widely accepted until science identified the single proven cause of the disease: the tubercle bacillus. Today there is a popular theory to explain cancer, heart disease, stroke, and other diseases about which science is still largely ignorant. The theory is that people become ill because they do not live right. They do not practice such basic health habits as eating breakfast, exercising regularly, not smoking, and not drinking to excess. In fact, however, there is no conclusive scientific evidence that keeping fit will ward off deadly diseases or add years to one's life. Yet people will continue to believe in "magic" explanations and solutions until science comes in with the cold, hard facts.

A summary of a book appears as part of the report on page 145.

Activities

1 Review the chapter carefully. Then, without looking back, answer the following questions.

1. True or false: _____ A summary is also known as a *précis* or *abstract*.

2. The length of a summary depends on:
   a. Its purpose
   b. The length of the original work
   c. The nature of the assignment
   d. All of the above

3. The first step in doing a summary is to:
   a. Preview the work   c. Read the work carefully
   b. Take notes on the work d. None of the above

4. Very often a magazine article will have not just a title but also a _____ that provides a brief summary of the material.

5. When previewing a book, look at the _____, which may summarize the main ideas developed in the book and describe briefly how the book is organized.

2 In a weekly magazine, read several different articles. Then write a one-paragraph summary of one of them.

Provide identifying information about the article and, in your own words, summarize the main point of the article and the key details used to support or develop that point. You may, if you like, quote briefly from the article. Be sure to enclose any sentences you borrow in quotation marks.

3 With the help of the *Readers' Guide to Periodical Literature,* locate in your library an article on one of the subjects listed on page 160. Then write a single-paragraph summary of the article. Follow the suggestions in 2 above.

4 In a monthly magazine, read two full-length articles of interest to you. Then write a several-paragraph summary of one of the articles. Follow the suggestions in 2 above.

5 Write a several-paragraph summary of a chapter from one of your textbooks. Try to choose a general interest subject such as psychology or sociology rather than a highly specialized field such as anatomy or electronics. In your summary, provide the necessary identifying information and present clearly several main ideas from the chapter, along with the key details that support or develop those points. You may quote some sentences from the book, but they should be only a small part of your report. Follow the suggestions in 2 above.

6 Watch a television show. Then prepare a summary of the show. In your first sentence, give basic information about the show by using a format such as the following: "The March 19, 1980, broadcast of CBS' *Sixty Minutes* examined. . . ."

10

Preparing a Report

This chapter will show you how to write a report that:

- Summarizes the assigned material
- Gives your reaction to the material

Each semester, you will probably be asked by at least one instructor to read a book or an article (or watch a TV show or a film) and to write a paper recording your response to the material. In these reports or reaction papers, your instructor will most likely expect you to do two things: *summarize the material* and *detail your reaction* to it. The following pages explain both parts of a report.

PART 1 OF A REPORT: A SUMMARY OF THE WORK

To develop the first part of a report, do the following:

1   Identify the author and title of the work and include in parentheses the publisher and publication date. For magazines, give the name of the magazine and the date of publication. (For TV shows and movies, provide the release date and the name of the network or studio.) Put this identifying information near the beginning of the paper.

2   Write an informative summary of the material. Condense the content of the work by highlighting its main points and key supporting points. (See pages 135 to 137 for a complete discussion of summarizing techniques.) Use direct quotations from the work to illustrate important ideas. (Refer to page 172 for ways to incorporate quoted material into the body of a paper.)

   Do not discuss in great detail any single aspect of the work and neglect to mention other equally important points. Summarize the material so that the reader gets a general sense of *all* key aspects of the original work. Also, keep the summary objective and factual. Do not include in the first part of the paper your personal reaction to the work; your subjective impression will form the basis of the second part of the paper.

Note: Some instructors will want you to make brief judgments about the work in the summary section of the paper. For example, you might be asked to comment briefly on the importance of the points made and the clarity of the overall structure. If this is the case, the first part of your paper will be an *evaluative* rather than an *informative* summary. The sentences below illustrate the difference between informative and evaluative summary statements. The italicized words in the second sentence demonstrate how a purely objective condensation of material can be turned into a subjective evaluation of the same content.

• Zimbardo explains that there are various degrees of shyness and that shyness means different things to different people.

- *With sensitivity and compassion,* Zimbardo explains that there are various degrees of shyness and that shyness means different things to different people.

   If you write an evaluative summary, be careful that you do not become so involved with making subjective statements that you forget to summarize the material. Remember, the first part of a report *must* give the reader a general sense of the work—even if you write an evaluative rather than an informative summary.

PART 2 OF A REPORT: YOUR REACTION TO THE WORK

To develop the second part of a report, do the following:

1 Focus on any or all of the questions listed below. (Check with your instructors to see if they want you to emphasize specific points.)
   a. How is the assigned work related to ideas and concerns discussed in the course for which you are preparing the paper? For example, what points made in the course textbook, class discussions, or lectures are treated more fully in the work?
   b. How is the work related to problems in our present-day world?
   c. How is the material related to your life, experiences, feelings, and ideas? For example, what emotions did the work arouse in you? Did the work increase your understanding of a particular issue? Did it change your perspective in any way?

2 Evaluate the merit of the work: the importance of its points, its accuracy, completeness, organization, and so on. You also should indicate here whether or not you would recommend the work to others, and why.

   Note: If you wrote an evaluative summary for the first part of the paper, do not repeat points already made there when you give your reaction in the second part. One way to avoid such an overlap is to limit your discussion in the second section to *specific* aspects of the work and deal only with *general* points in the evaluative summary at the beginning of the paper.

POINTS TO KEEP IN MIND WHEN WRITING THE REPORT

Here are some important matters to consider as you prepare the report.

1 Apply the four basic standards of effective writing (unity, support, organization, and clear, error-free sentences—see pages 117 to 126) when writing the report.

a. Make sure each major paragraph presents and then develops a single main idea. This central thought is expressed in a main-idea sentence or topic sentence. For example, in the model report, each paragraph after the short introductory paragraph takes on and develops a different major point. The second paragraph summarizes the distinguishing traits of shy people and the results of those traits. The third paragraph summarizes the ways to dispel shyness. In the fourth paragraph, a parallel is drawn between the student writer's experience in school and the student's description of the fierce competition that breeds shyness. Similarly, the fifth and sixth paragraphs develop single points. The student writer then closes the report with a short concluding paragraph.

b. Support any general points or attitudes you express with specific reasons and details. Statements such as "I agreed with many ideas in this article" or "I found the book very interesting" are meaningless without specific evidence that shows why you feel as you do. Look at the model report closely to see the way the main idea of each major paragraph is developed by specific supporting evidence.

c. Organize the material in the paper. Follow the basic *plan of organization* in the model report: an introduction, a summary of one or more paragraphs, a reaction of two or more paragraphs, and a conclusion. Use *connecting words* to make clear relationships among ideas in the paper. For example, note how the connecting words *First, Second, Next,* and *Finally* are used to introduce the sequence of points in the third paragraph. Provide *linking sentences* wherever possible between sections of the paper. Note, for instance, how the topic sentence in the sixth paragraph refers to the content of the preceding paragraph while also introducing the content of the new paragraph. There are other linking sentences as well in the paper.

d. Proofread the paper carefully for errors in grammar, punctuation, and spelling. The model report is free of such errors.

2 Identify any additional works you mention in the paper in the same way you identified the primary work. For example, in the fifth paragraph of the report, information about the books *A Survey of the Social Sciences* and *Adolescent Development* is enclosed in parentheses.

3 Document quotations from all works by placing the page number in parentheses after the quoted material. Look at the second,

third, and fifth paragraphs of the report for an illustration of this procedure. You may use quotations in the summary and reaction parts of the paper, but do not overly rely on them. Use them only to emphasize key points.

A MODEL REPORT

Here is a report written by a student in an educational psychology course. Look at the paper closely to see how it follows the guidelines for report writing described in this chapter.

A REPORT ON PHILIP ZIMBARDO'S *SHYNESS*

PART 1: SUMMARY

Introductory paragraph

In *Shyness* (Reading, Massachusetts: Addison-Wesley Publishing Company, 1977), Philip Zimbardo analyzes a widespread but little understood personality trait—shyness. The book is divided into two sections: what shyness is and what can be done about it.

Topic sentence for first summarizing paragraph

Zimbardo spends most of Part I describing the traits that characterize shy people as well as the consequences of these traits. Shy people are fearful of situations they perceive as threatening. Also, they are excessively preoccupied with themselves and are overly concerned with being evaluated negatively. As a result of these feelings, most shy people are alienated. They feel they must "avoid any situation that may be potentially embarrassing, thereby further isolating themselves from other people and instead concentrating on their own shortcomings" (29). Because shy people tend to retreat, they passively accept the world as it is and so force themselves into a kind of powerlessness.

Topic sentence for second summarizing paragraph

In Part II, Zimbardo shows that there are a number of ways to dispel shyness. First, he describes a number of activities to help shy people develop a more realistic sense of themselves. Second, he presents various exercises to help shy people develop their self-esteem and acquire much needed social skills. Next, he outlines strategies that can be used to help children, students, and mates overcome shyness. Finally, Zimbardo discusses the changes that must be made to correct society's "overemphasis on competition and individual achievement" (51).

PART 2: REACTION

Topic sentence for first reaction paragraph

I reacted strongly to Zimbardo's description of the conditions in society that create shyness. I, for one, often felt overwhelmed by the fierce competition that went on in school. Even in kindergarten, show-and-tell was a battle among 5-year-olds. Each of us hoped to beat out the rest of the class by bringing in the best, most interesting item. This competition to win, to be best, was repeated with increasing urgency throughout grade school. Who would be in the highest group? Who would win the spelling bee? Who would get the highest mark on the arithmetic test? These questions seemed to haunt our young lives. To win—often at the expense of others—that's what we are taught. No wonder so many of us become fearful and anxious to achieve.

Topic sentence for second reaction paragraph

I look back at those tension-filled years with sadness. I know now that school shouldn't frighten children and undermine their confidence. Rather, school should help children develop a strong, positive sense of self. In fact, our two class texts, as well as Zimbardo's book, take the same position. For example, in *A Survey of the Social Sciences* (New York: McGraw-Hill, 1975), Gary and Duane Brown argue that education must "function in the area of personal development." (53). Elizabeth Hurlock makes the same point in *Adolescent Development* (New York: McGraw-Hill, 1973) when she quotes this statement made by J. C. Solomon: "The schoolroom must be looked upon as a force secondary in importance to the home in the development of human personality" (332). These authors' views parallel one of Zimbardo's key points. He writes that children must be accepted for who they are, not for what they accomplish. They "need to feel that home and school are safe places, places where they are recognized for their personal worth . . . , where their uniqueness is cherished" (66). Zimbardo then goes on to say that teachers must create a supportive environment in which children take risks and discover the richness of their inner resources.

Topic sentence for third reaction paragraph

Zimbardo's account of the conditions which bring about students' growth remind me of our November 3 class discussion about Carl Rogers' theory of teaching. Rogers advocates the creation of nonthreatening, student-centered classrooms. The teachers in such classrooms demonstrate unconditional positive regard for youngsters and empathic understanding of how children feel. Equally important, teachers provide a rich array of resources that encourage children to experiment, to become comfortable with themselves and with others. In such an environment, Rogers believes, children become more self-accepting and develop more flexible and adaptive attitudes and behaviors; they are liberated from the inhibiting, shyness-generating effects of competition.

Concluding paragraph

Many people, I feel, would profit from reading Zimbardo's book: shy people as well as people with withdrawn friends, spouses, children, or relatives.

But teachers, most of all, would find the book invaluable. Zimbardo has done more than merely examine the origins and consequences of shyness. He shows what all of us, especially teachers, can do to ease the pain of shyness. With sensitivity and a real sense of the practical, he shows that shy children can grow. If they have the support of caring adults, they can develop the skills and attitudes needed to become strong, confident individuals.

Activities

1 Review the chapter carefully. Then, without looking back, answer the following questions.

1. A report usually consists of a summary and a _____.

2. True or false: _____ You should provide identifying information about the work at the close of your report.

3. In the reaction part of a report, you can show how the work relates to:
   a. Ideas discussed in the course for which you are preparing the paper
   b. Problems in our present-day world
   c. Your own life, experiences, feelings, and ideas
   d. All of the above

4. The basic plan of organization for a report consists in an _____, a summary of one or more paragraphs, a reaction of two or more paragraphs, and a _____ _____.

5. A statement such as "I found the book very interesting" is meaningless without _____.

2 Read a magazine article that interests you. Then write a report on the article and include the following: (1) an introductory paragraph which provides the necessary identifying information, (2) a one-paragraph summary of the article, (3) one or more paragraphs reacting to the article, and (4) a brief concluding paragraph. You may, if you like, quote briefly from the article. Be sure to enclose the words that you take from the article in quotation marks and put the page number in parentheses at the end of the quoted material.

3 Read a book that your instructor suggests and then write a report on it. Include a summary of at least one paragraph and a reaction of two or more paragraphs. Prepare an introduction (include identifying information) and a conclusion. Also, make sure that each major paragraph in your report develops a single main idea. You may quote some sentences from the book, but they should be only a small part of your report. Follow the directions in 2 above when you quote material.

11

Using the Library

This chapter will show you how to use the library and its:

- Main desk
- Card catalog
- Stacks
- Reference section
- Periodical area

A surprising number of students seem overwhelmed by their college libraries. They don't understand how the library is set up and so are not sure how to use its many services. If you share these students' confusion, this chapter will help you. It will provide the basic information you need to use your college library with confidence.

Libraries vary in size, layout, and the services they offer. Most libraries, however, have a *main desk,* a *card catalog, stacks,* a *reference section,* and a *periodical area.* Each of these will be discussed on the pages that follow.

THE MAIN DESK

The main desk, often located in a central spot, is usually staffed by at least one professional librarian and several assistants. Check with the staff to see if there are any brochures or pamphlets that describe the layout and services of the library. Many college libraries give tours of the facilities, particularly at the beginning of the school year. If descriptive pamphlets or tours are available, take advantage of them. The more familiar you are with the library, the more effectively you will be able to use it.

Many libraries provide the following services: interlibrary loan system; copying machines; typing facilities; study carrels; record and film collections; a vertical file containing pamphlets and clippings; a government document room; and microfilm and microfiche files for out-of-date newspapers, magazines, and the like. Check with the main desk to find out which of these services are available.

Instructors often put materials that many students will use on reserve. These materials must usually be kept in the library, although as times they may be taken out overnight. Books on reserve are often shelved behind the main desk.

THE CARD CATALOG

Author, Title, and Subject Cards

The card catalog is a file of cards alphabetically arranged in drawers; it lists all the books in the library. You can find out whether the library has a certain book and where it is located by looking it up in the card catalog according to title, author, or subject.

For example, if you wanted to see if the library had *Freedom to Learn* by Carl Rogers, you could look up the author's name under *R* (Rogers) in the *Authors* section of the card catalog. Or you could look up *Freedom to Learn* under *F* in the *Titles* section of the catalog. Or you could look it up under the category of "Education" in the *Subjects* section of the catalog.

Shown below are subject, title, and author cards for a single book. Note carefully the kinds of information provided on the author card and how the information is presented.

SUBJECT CARD

ADULTHOOD.

HQ   Sheehy, Gail.
1064   Passages : predictable crises of a–
.U5   dult life / Gail Sheehy. -- 1st ed. --
S522   New York : Dutton, c1976.

TITLE CARD

Passages; predictable crises of
adult life

HQ   Sheehy, Gail.
1064   Passages : predictable crises of a –
.U5   dult life / Gail Sheehy. -- 1 st ed. --
S522   New York : Dutton, c1976.

AUTHOR CARD

Author ——————————→ Sheehy, Gail.

Call number (how to → HQ   →Passages : predictable crises of a–
find the book)   1064   dult life / Gail Sheehy. -- 1st ed. --
                          .U5   New York : Dutton, c1976.
Title   S522   xiv, 393 p. ; 25 cm.

                                   Bibliography: p. 375–381.
Place of publication,   Includes index.
publisher, and year
of publication

Subject headings   →1. Adulthood. 2. Maturation (Psychol–
(Refer to these   ogy). 3. Socialization. 4. Middle age.
headings in the   5. United States -- Social conditions
card catalog to   -- 1960–
find related   I. Title.
books.)

                                   HQ1064.U5S522   301.43′4   76–4907
                                                               MARC

• Activities on the card catalog are on pages 158 and 159.

Call Numbers

The call numbers, printed in the upper left-hand corner of each card, tell you where a book is located. The call number, as distinctive as a social security number, is also printed on the spine of every book in the library. Materials are shelved according to their call numbers, making it possible to arrange books systematically and so find them easily. Many libraries have near the main desk a floor plan which shows in what sections of the library different call numbers can be found.

The two most common classification systems are the Dewey decimal and Library of Congress systems.

The Dewey decimal system divides all books into ten major categories:

000–099	General Works	600–699	Technology (Applied
100–199	Philosophy		Sciences)
200–299	Religion	700–799	The Arts
300–399	Social Sciences	800–899	Literature
400–499	Language	900–999	History
500–599	Pure Science		

The Library of Congress system, the one used by most college libraries, divides books into twenty-one categories:

A	General Works and Polygraphy	L	Education
B	Philosophy and Religion	M	Music
C	History and Auxiliary Sciences	N	Fine Arts
D	History and Topography (excluding America)	P	Language and Literature
		Q	Science
E–F	America	R	Medicine
G	Geography and Anthropology	S	Agriculture and Plant and Animal Husbandry
H	Social Sciences	T	Technology
J	Political Science	U	Military Science
K	Law	V	Naval Science
		Z	Bibliography and Library Science

Hints about Using the Card Catalog

You may at times have trouble locating material in the card catalog because you are not familiar with some of the conventions most libraries follow when filing cards. Keeping the following points in mind should make it easier for you to find the information you need.

1   Books are not alphabetized using *A, An, The* when they are the first words in a title. Instead, the book is cataloged according to the second word in the title. For example, the book *The Heart of the Matter* would be found under *Heart*.

2   You will often find that cards have additional words or abbreviations written above the call number. You may, for instance, find such designations as *Ref, Reserve, Spec Coll.* These designations means, respectively, that these books will be found in the *reference room,* at the *reserve desk,* and in the *special collections room.* You will not find these materials in the stacks.

3   Near the bottom of many cards in the catalog, you will find a number of headings. For example, on the card shown on page 151, there are three headings: "1. Adulthood. 2. Maturation (Psychology). 3. Socialization. 4. Middle Age. 5. United States—Social conditions—1960—." These headings tell you the subject areas in the card catalog under which the book in question is filed. You can refer to these subject areas for related books on your topic.

THE STACKS

The stacks are the library shelves where books are arranged according to their call numbers. In a library having open stacks (ones that you are permitted to enter), follow these steps to find a book. If, for example, you are looking for *Freedom to Learn* by Carl Rogers, you first use the card catalog to get the call number, which is LB1051/R636 in the Library of Congress system. (Libraries using the Dewey decimal system have call letters made up entirely of numbers rather than letters and numbers. However, you use the same basic method to locate a book.) Then you go to the section of the stacks that holds the *L*s. After you locate the *L*s, you look for the *LB*s. After that, you look for LB1051. Then you look for LB1051/R. Finally, you look for LB1051/R636, and you have the book.

   If the library has closed stacks, you will have to make out a call slip, supplying the call number and other identifying information about the book. A staff person will then locate the book and bring it to you.

   • Activities on the stacks are on page 159.

THE REFERENCE SECTION

The reference section stocks such general resource materials as encyclopedias, atlases, and yearbooks. People sometimes conduct their preliminary research here before going to the card catalog for more specific materials. Resources in the reference section are generally large, expensive volumes and so cannot be taken out of the library. They usually must be used on the premises.

It would be impractical to give here all the reference materials carried by even a small library, and so only a brief list of such materials has been provided.

Atlases
Hammond Medallion World Atlas
National Atlas of the United States

Biographical References
Biography Index: A Cumulative Index to Biographical Material in Books and Magazines
Current Biography: Who's News and Why
Who's Who

Yearbooks
Guiness Book of World Records
Information Please Almanac
The World Almanac and Book of Facts

Bibliographies
Bibliographic Index: A Cumulative Bibliography of Bibliographies
Books in Print: The Cumulative Book Index

References in Biology
Biological Abstracts
A Dictionary of Biological Terms
The Encyclopedia of Biological Sciences

References in Chemistry, Physics, and Math
Chemical Abstracts
Handbook of Chemistry and Physics
Mathematics Dictionary

References in Education
Current Index to Journals in Education
Education Index
ERIC Research in Education

References in Literature
Book Review Digest
Bibliographical Guide to the Study of the Literature of the U.S.A.
A Handbook to Literature

References in Political Science
American Political Science Review
Dictionary of American Politics
Public Affairs Information Service

References in Psychology
American Journal of Psychology
A Dictionary of Psychology
Psychology Abstracts

References in Sociology
American Journal of Sociology
American Sociological Review
Sociological Abstracts

References in Theater
Index to Plays in Collections
Play Index

Dictionaries of Quotations
Dictionary of Quotations
Familiar Quotations

Encyclopedias
Colliers Encyclopedia
Encyclopedia Americana
Encyclopaedia Britannica

Government Publications
Guide to U.S. Government Serials and Periodicals
Monthly Catalogue of U.S. Government Publications
Vertical File Index

References in Art
Art Index
Guide to Art Reference Books

References in Business
Business Periodicals Index
Encyclopedia of Banking and Finance
Sources of Business Information

References in Engineering
Engineering Index Monthly
Sources of Engineering Information

References in History
American Historical Review
Historical Abstracts

References in Music and Dance
Dance Encyclopedia
Dictionary of Music and Musicians

References in Philosophy
The Encyclopedia of Philosophy
Journal of Philosophy

References in Religion
Index to Religious Periodical Literature
A Reader's Guide to the Great Religions

References in Social Sciences
A Reader's Guide to the Social Sciences
Social Sciences and Humanities
Sources of Information in the Social Sciences: A Guide to the Literature

THE PERIODICAL AREA

Periodicals are magazines, journals, and newspapers that are printed at periodic (regular or intermittent) intervals during the year. Because these materials contain current information, they are often particularly valuable when doing research. Just as you can use the card catalog to locate a specific book, so you can use one of several periodical guides or indexes to locate a specific article in a magazine or other publication.

The *Readers' Guide*

The most common of these indexes is the *Readers' Guide to Periodical Literature*. This guide lists articles in over one hundred popular magazines, such as *Newsweek, Time,* and *The Reader's Digest,* as well as more specialized magazines, such as *Retirement Living, Ebony, National Review,* and *Science Digest.* Articles are listed under both subject and author. If, for example, you wanted to learn the names of articles published on the subject of running, you would look under the heading "RUNNING." If you wanted to identify articles written by Ralph Nader, you would look under his last name.

Some students are confused by the format used to present information in the *Readers' Guide.* However, all the abbreviations used in an entry are explained at the front of each issue. Here, for example, is a typical entry:

Subject heading

RUNNING

Title of article   Author of article   Illustrated

What makes Linda run? J. F. Fixx. il

Fam Health 10:24-4 Ap'78

Name of   Volume   Page   Date
magazine   number   numbers

Note the sequence in which information is given about the article:

1. The subject heading (or author, last name first) in capitals.
2. The title of the article.
3. The author (if it is a signed article).
4. Whether the article has a bibliography (*bibl*) or not, or is illustrated (*il*) or not. Other abbreviations are shown in the front of any issue of the *Readers' Guide.*
5. The name of the magazine. The magazine abbreviated in the entry is *Family Health.* Refer to the list of magazines in the front of the index to identify other abbreviations.
6. The volume number of the magazine (preceding the colon).
7. The page numbers on which the article appears (after the colon).
8. The date when the article appeared. Dates are abbreviated: for example, *Ag* stands for *August, S* for *September.* Other abbreviations for months are shown at the front of any issue of the *Readers' Guide.*

- Activities on the *Readers' Guide* are on pages 159 and 160.

Other Indexes

If you are doing research in a specialized area, your instructor or a librarian should be able to tell you whether one of the specialized indexes listed below will be a helpful source of information.

Applied Science and Technology Index

Art Index

Book Review Digest

Business Periodical Index

Education Index

Nursing Index

Social Sciences and Humanities Index

Essay and General Literature Index

New York Times Index

Public Affairs Information Service

Entries in the specialized indexes follow roughly the same format as that used in the *Readers' Guide.* If you have trouble understanding an entry, refer to the guide at the front of the index for an explanation of the symbols used.

The File of Periodical Holdings

After using the appropriate index to identify articles you would like to read, you need to determine (1) if the library receives the periodicals you want, (2) whether it has the particular issues you want, and (3) where in the library the periodicals can be found. For this information, check the file (sometimes a booklet) of periodical holdings; the file is located in the periodical area.

Most libraries provide an explanatory key so you can interpret the information entered in the periodical holding file. This key will tell you whether a particular magazine is on microfilm or microfiche or is available in loose or bound copies.

A Final Note about Periodicals

Current issues of magazines and journals remain unbound and are usually shelved on open stacks in the periodical area. Back issues, however, are bound in annual or semiannual volumes and may be in the periodical area or in some other spot in the library. Most libraries keep loose copies of selected recent newspapers on open stacks in the periodical area. Past issues of particularly important newspapers may be on microfilm. Check with the library staff for the location of these materials.

Activities

1 Review the chapter carefully. Then, without looking back, answer the following questions.

1. Books placed on reserve by instructors are often shelved near the:
   a. Stacks   c. Periodical area
   b. Main desk   d. Reference section

2. A card catalog usually indexes books according to:
   a. Author   c. Subject
   b. Title   d. All of the above

3. To locate a book in the stacks, you need to know its _____ _____ .

4. Periodicals are:
   a. Books   c. Magazines
   b. Card files   d. All of the above

5. True or false: _____ To find out whether a library has the specific issue of the magazine you want, you should check the file of periodical holdings.

2 Use the library card catalog to answer the following questions. Put your answers on a separate sheet of paper.

1. What is the title of one book by John Kenneth Galbraith listed under his name (listings appear under the author's last name)?

2. What is the title of a book by Betty Friedan?

3. Who is the author of *The Good Earth?* (*Note:* Do not look up a book's title under *The, A,* or *An,* but the word following—in this case, *Good*).

4. Who is the author of *Manchild in the Promised Land?*

5. List three books and their authors dealing with the subject of nutrition.

6. List three books and their authors dealing with the subject of adoption.

7. Look up a book titled *Silent Spring* or *The Hidden Persuaders* or *The Immense Journey* and give the following information:
   * Author
   * Place of publication
   * Publishers
   * Date of publication
   * Subject headings at the bottom of the card
   * Call number

8. Look up a book written by Abraham Maslow or Margaret Mead or David Riesman and give the following information:
   * Title
   * Place of publication
   * Publisher
   * Date of publication
   * Subject headings at the bottom of the card
   * Call number

3 Use the library stacks to answer the following questions on a separate sheet of paper. (*Note:* The questions assume that your library classifies books according to the Library of Congress system.)

1. What author is the subject of the books that fall between PS1850 and PS1888?

2. What is the general subject of the books that fall between D727 and D821?

3. What is the general subject of the books that fall between HQ1115 and HQ1870?

4. What country is the subject of the books that fall between DK1 and DK399?

5. What is the general subject of the books that fall between QA90 and QA950?

4 Use the *Readers' Guide to Periodical Literature* to look up recent articles on (1) capital punishment, (2) insomnia, and (3) marriage. On a separate sheet of paper, record the following information about each article:

* Article title
* Author (if given)
* Name of magazine
* Volume
* Page(s)

5   Use the library to do some preliminary research on a subject that interests you. Choose one of the areas below:

Handicapped children	Feminism
Gun control	Gardening
Photography	Prison reform
Insect control	Drug abuse
Dinosaurs	Martin Luther King
Juvenile delinquency	Antibiotics
Hay fever	Acupuncture
Extrasensory perception	UFOs

Research the topic first through the *Subjects* section of the catalog and then in the periodical indexes named below. On a separate sheet of paper, provide the following information:

1. The topic

2. Five books on the topic; include these items:
   - Author
   - Title
   - Place of publication
   - Publisher
   - Date of publication

3. Three articles on the topic from the *Readers' Guide to Periodical Literature*. Include these items:
   - Title of article
   - Author (if given)
   - Title of periodical
   - Volume
   - Page(s)
   - Date

4. Three articles on the topic from other indexes (*New York Times Index* or *Social Science and Humanities Index* or *Essay and General Literature Index* and others). Include these items:
   - Title of article
   - Author (if given)
   - Title of periodical
   - Volume
   - Page(s)
   - Date

6   Make up a floor plan of your college library. Label the main desk, card catalog, stacks, reference section, and periodical area.

On the floor plan, indicate where in the library you will find the following materials. Use the abbreviations in parentheses to indicate where the material can be found.

- *Readers' Guide to Periodical Literature (RG)*
- *Encyclopaedia Britannica (EB)*
- Current magazines (CM)
- Microfilms (M)
- File of periodical holdings (FPH)

7 On separate paper, answer the following questions about your college library.

1. What are the library's hours during the week and on the weekend?

2. For how long may books be taken out?

3. What kind of identification do you need to take out a book?

4. What's the fine on overdue books?

5. Is the Dewey decimal or Library of Congress system used to catalog books?

6. Are the stacks open or closed?

7. Are there any study carrels? Where are they?

8. Are there any typewriters? Where are they?

9. Are there any copying facilities? Where are they?

10. Are there any special collections in the library? Where are they?

11. Is there a reserve desk? Where is it?

12

Writing

the Research Paper

This chapter will show you how to write a research paper by:

- Selecting an area to research
- Taking notes on the material
- Organizing the notes
- Preparing and revising drafts of the paper
- Using an accepted format in the paper

Instructors in a number of subjects will probably ask you to write research papers as part of their course requirements. Depending on the course and instructor, you may be asked to *make and defend a point of some kind*. For example, your concern in the paper might be to provide evidence for your belief that gambling should be legalized. Or you may simply be required to *present information about a particular subject*. For instance, the assignment might be to explain several psychologists' theories about the stages of development in children. In either case, you are doing a research project.

Here is a summary of the steps to take if you want to write an effective research paper.

1. Select and then narrow your research area
2. Prepare a working purpose and outline
3. Prepare a working bibliography
4. Take notes to support the working purpose and develop the working outline
5. Organize the note cards
6. Write a thesis statement and prepare a final outline
7. Write most of the first draft
8. Complete and revise the first draft
9. Prepare the first draft of the footnotes and bibliography
10. Assemble the final paper

The rest of this chapter explains and illustrates each of these different steps in writing a research paper. By following these guidelines, you can be confident of having the skills needed to write an effective, academically sound paper.

Be sure to review Chapter 11 ("Using the Library") before reading this chapter. You must know how to use the information resources in the library before you can carry out a research project.

STEP 1   SELECT AND THEN NARROW YOUR RESEARCH AREA

The best area to research is one that interests you. At the same time, you must make sure your library has sufficient information on the area. You should, then, go to the *Subjects* section of the library card catalog and see whether there are at least four books on your general topic. For example, if you initially choose the general area of adoption, you should find at least four books listed on adoption. In addition, check the library stacks to make sure that the books are available on the shelves.

You should also go through a recent volume of the *Readers' Guide to Periodical Literature* or the appropriate specialized periodical index to see whether articles are listed on your subject. Then check the file of periodical holdings (you may have to ask a library assistant to point out the file) to see if the library actually has the periodicals you need. It might be helpful, too, to look up articles on the subject in an encyclopedia.

If you can find several books and articles, then pursue your research area. Otherwise, you may have to choose another area. You cannot write a paper on a subject for which research materials are not available. Do not take notes at this stage. All you are trying to do is survey a broad area to determine how much information is available and whether the subject interests you enough to spend time researching it.

Read about the general area until you identify a specific aspect that you would like to explore further. Here is the way several students progressively narrowed the general areas they started to research:

	General Area	Less General Area	Specific Topic
Student 1	Vietnam war	Vietnam veterans	Problems of veterans disabled in Vietnam war
Student 2	Colleges	Decline in college enrollment	Ways colleges are dealing with declining enrollments
Student 3	Inflation	Easy credit	Abuse of credit cards
Student 4	The family	High divorce rate	Divorce rate among teens
Student 5	Computers	Data banks	Medical data banks

STEP 2 PREPARE A WORKING PURPOSE AND OUTLINE

You should prepare a working purpose to guide your research of the specific topic. To define your working purpose, ask yourself these questions: What do I want my paper to demonstrate? Based upon my preliminary reading, what statement do I want to make about my topic? Your answer to these questions becomes the working purpose of your paper.

Write the purpose in one or several sentences. Here is the way the students above moved from a specific topic to a working purpose:

	Specific Topic	Working Purpose
Student 1	Problems of veterans disabled in Vietnam war	To show that disabled veterans of the Vietnam war faced many problems when they returned home
Student 2	Ways colleges are dealing with declining enrollment	To show that some colleges are bolstering their enrollments by offering programs that attract new groups of students
Student 3	Abuse of credit cards	To show that overreliance on credit cards poses difficulties for many people
Student 4	Divorce rate among teens	To show that educational programs can help young people develop more realistic views of marriage
Student 5	Medical data banks	To show that the storing of medical information in data banks can create serious problems

Once you have identified your working purpose, your job becomes much more focused. You look for materials that develop your working purpose. You have a reason for using some resources and not others.

Prepare a working outline of your paper. The outline is not a formal one. Rather, it is broad and brief and indicates what you think, in this early stage of your research, will be the major sections of the paper. Like the working purpose, the working outline helps direct your efforts because you limit your reading primarily to those materials which develop the major sections you have outlined.

Here is the working outline prepared by student 5 mentioned above. Note two things: first, the outline is headed by the working purpose and, second, major categories do not, at this point, have to be divided into subcategories. Main headings are sufficient.

Working Purpose and Outline

To show that the storing of confidential medical information in data banks can create serious problems.

    I. Questionable ways medical information is collected
   II. Medical information used for nonmedical purposes
  III. Difficulty people have gaining access to their own records

STEP 3 PREPARE A WORKING BIBLIOGRAPHY

A working bibliography is a list of sources on your subject. Preparing a working bibliography helps you identify books and articles particularly relevant to your topic. These should be the first materials you read.

Use a separate 3 × 5 or 4 × 6 inch card to list each source you have used or think you will use as you research your topic. Refer to the following sources to gather material for the working bibliography:

- The *Subjects* cards in the card catalog
- The *Readers' Guide to Periodical Literature*
- Specialized periodical indexes
- The pamphlet file (you may have to ask a library assistant to tell you where this file is located)

Include on each card the information listed below:

For Books	For Articles
Author (last name first)	Author (last name first)
Title (underlined)	Title of article (enclosed in quotation marks)
Place of publication	
Publisher	Title of periodical (underlined)
Date of publication	Volume (if available)
Call number (upper right-hand corner)	Pages
	Date

Here are copies of bibliography cards for a book and a magazine article:

```
                                          R864
                                          W74
    Westin, Alan F.
    Computers, Health Records, and
          Citizens' Rights
    Washington, D.C.
    U.S. Government Printing Office, 1976
```

```
       Britten, Ann H.
       "Rights to Privacy in Medical Records"
       The Journal of Legal Medicine
       Pages 30-37
       July/August 1975
```

STEP 4 READ ABOUT YOUR TOPIC AND TAKE NOTES

Now you are ready to take notes that develop your working purpose and working outline. Be sure to stay on track; do not let yourself become sidetracked by interesting but irrelevant material.

Follow these guidelines when taking notes:

- Use 3 × 5 or 4 × 6 inch cards. You will find it much easier to organize and categorize your notes (see step 5) if they are written on cards rather than on sheets of paper.
- Write on one side of the card only.
- Put only one kind of information, from one source, on any one card. For example, the sample card below has information on one idea (the difficulty of getting investigative agencies to police their own practices) from one source (Hayden's article in *Civil Liberties Review*):

> The activities of private investigative agencies are supposed to be controlled by the Fair Credit Report Act of 1970. However, because the industry was primarily responsible for preparing these guidelines, there isn't a rigorous enforcement of the regulations.
>
> Hayden, <u>Civil Liberties</u>, 24

- Be sure to include identifying information at the bottom of each card: the author's last name, a shortened version of the title, and page number.

When you take notes, you may quote directly, summarize in your own words, or combine the two.* Put quotation marks around all material which you take word for word from any source. If you omit material from a quoted passage, show the omission (ellipses) by using three spaced periods (. . .). When the omission is from the end of a quoted sentence, use four dots (. . . .), with the fourth dot indicating the period at the end of the sentence. If you add a word or two to make the meaning of a quotation clear, put brackets around the added

---

* There is one other kind of note you may want to take. If you have any insight into the organization or development of your paper, record those ideas on a separate note card and put the word "Me" in the upper right-hand corner.

material. In a summary, you condense the original by stating its main points briefly in your own words. When you take notes, you should usually try to summarize in your own words rather than quote.

Here is a copy of a note card that combines both summary and direct quotation:

Many representatives of the health insurance industry claim that people do not have strong concerns about the confidentiality of their medical records. However, a study by Dr. Catherine Rosen at a mental health center in Georgia "provides striking proof of what civil libertarians have been asserting—that . . . millions of persons . . . do care about the circulation of their personal data. . . ."

Westin, Computers, 245

Be careful when summarizing not to stay too close to the phrasing of the original. Otherwise, you will be stealing (the formal term is *plagiarizing*—using someone else's work as your own). Here is a way to avoid plagiarizing. As soon as you come across material you want to use in a paper, close the book or article. Use your memory to restate the important points in the material and then write the ideas down on a card, using your own words. Do not open the book or article until you have completed the card or unless you want to quote something directly. Also, when you summarize or quote, be sure to record on a card the exact source and page from which you take each piece of information. In this way, you will not forget that you have borrowed the material.

STEP 5 ORGANIZE THE NOTE CARDS

Keeping your working purpose in mind, go through your note cards and group them into distinct categories. Put all the cards relating to a single major category together in one stack. The number of main categories you identify will determine how many stacks of cards you have.

At the top of each card, write a label or heading that summarizes the content of the card. This heading will help you organize the information you have gathered on your topic.

Decide the order in which you will probably use the major categories in your paper. These are some ordering principles to consider: less to more important, problem to solution, grouping related ideas together, time sequence, cause and effect, effect and cause, specific to general, and general to specific.

Although grouping and labeling note cards may be time-consuming, the activity is invaluable because it forces you to pull your thoughts together.

STEP 6 WRITE A THESIS STATEMENT AND PREPARE A FINAL OUTLINE

Write a thesis statement for your paper. The *thesis statement* expresses the central idea of your paper; it serves as a map to show the direction the paper will take. Spend the time needed to write an effective thesis. Without it, your work will lack the necessary focus. Here are several examples of how students moved from a working purpose to a thesis statement:

	Working Purpose	Thesis Statement
Student 1	To show that disabled veterans of the Vietnam war faced many problems when they returned home	Many disabled Vietnam veterans needing extensive physical and psychological treatment faced special problems dealing with the bureaucracy of the Veterans Administration.
Student 2	To show that some colleges are bolstering their enrollments by offering programs that attract new groups of students	Many colleges have dealt with the problem of declining enrollments by developing a number of specialized programs tailored to the needs of nontraditional students.
Student 3	To show that overreliance on credit cards poses difficulties for many people	In this era of easy plastic credit, unprecedented numbers of Americans face financial and emotional bankruptcy because they have overextended themselves.
Student 4	To show that educational programs can help young people develop more realistic views of marriage	Concerned about the failure of many teenage marriages, a number of school and religious organizations have designed programs to develop young people's awareness of the responsibilities of marriage.
Student 5	To show that the storing of medical information in data banks can create serious problems	Real concern has developed about potential abuses in the collection and storing of confidential medical information in centralized data banks.

Now prepare a final outline. The outline shows how the thesis statement will be developed in the paper through main points and key supporting points. Preparing the outline encourages you to organize your thoughts clearly and logically and so eases the actual writing you do in step 7. The final outline prepared for the model research paper is on page 178.

In the outline, use logical symbols (numbers and letters) to show a series of main points or supporting items under a main point. Always begin main points at the same spot on the margin and indent subpoints consistently under the main points. Use the following symbols to indicate the relationship among the various parts of an outline:

Roman numerals: I, II, III, etc.
   Capital letters: A, B, C, etc.
      Numbers: 1, 2, 3, etc.
         Small letters: a, b, c, etc.
            Numbers in parentheses: (1), (2), (3), etc.
               Small letters in parentheses: (a), (b), (c), etc.

Test the logic of the outline by asking yourself these questions:

- Is the thesis statement expressed clearly and precisely? Does it appear at the top of the outline?
- Do the main headings develop the thesis of the paper? Do they represent major sections of the report? Are they sequenced logically?
- Does each subheading develop the main heading under which it is found? Are the subheadings sequenced logically?

This brief checklist will help you identify weaknesses in the design of your paper—before you begin to write.

STEP 7   WRITE MOST OF THE FIRST DRAFT

Using your thesis statement, final outline, and labeled note cards, write the first draft of the paper. Although you do not need to prepare a finished product at this stage, your first draft should be substantial and well-thought-out. Anyone reading it should, without difficulty, understand the thesis of the paper and its main and supporting points.

Apply all that you know about the standards of unity, support, and organization (see pages 117 to 126). Concentrate especially on the first two standards. Ask yourself the following:

- Does each of the supporting paragraphs develop the thesis of the paper?
- Do the supporting paragraphs have topic sentences?
- Does the material in each supporting paragraph develop the topic sentence?

Do not, at this point, write an introduction and conclusion. Wait until step 8, when the body of the paper is written.

Whenever you borrow material, be sure to acknowledge your source. You *must* do this whether you quote directly or summarize ideas in your own words. To indicate your source, follow these guidelines:

- Every time you include in your paper material taken from one of your sources, put the shortened version of the title and page number in parentheses at the end of the borrowed material. If you fail to do this, you will be plagiarizing. (You will replace this temporary method for indicating sources with a formal footnote system in step 9.)
- You do not have to give your source if the information you present is *common knowledge.* Common knowledge may be defined as information most people would come across after reading two or three general resources about a subject. However, if you are in doubt whether or not to show a source, play it safe and do!

Now put away the first draft for several days. If this isn't possible, let at least several hours go by before you start revising the paper. The time lapse will allow you to evaluate what you have written with more objectivity.

STEP 8   COMPLETE AND REVISE THE FIRST DRAFT

This is the time to reread closely what you have written. Try to look at the first draft as though you were seeing it for the first time. The paper's thesis and main and supporting points should be clear.

Draft an introduction and conclusion for the paper. The introduction should capture the reader's interest and state the thesis of the paper. Refer to pages 129 and 130 for information on writing introductions. The conclusion should flow easily from the body of the paper and should signal to the reader that the paper is ending. See page 130 for more information on conclusions.

Now you are ready to revise all that you have written: the introduction, body, and conclusion. Do all the revising needed to ensure that your paper meets the four standards of *unity, support, organization,* and *clear, error-free sentences.* See pages 117 to 126 and the suggestions for polishing a paper on pages 130 and 131.

Pay close attention to parts of the paper in which you quote directly or summarize someone else's information in your own words. Follow these guidelines:

- Make sure you use quotation marks and ellipses correctly when you quote material word for word.
- Introduce or lead into a quotation and borrowed material as often as possible. For example, use these kinds of phrases: "According to Westin," "Westin believes that," "In Westin's opinion," "Westin states," "As Westin explains," and so on. Aim for variety in the openers you select.
- Punctuate and capitalize correctly when using quoted material in a paper. See the model research paper (pages 179 and 180) for ways to work a quotation into the text.

Next, read your revised paper out loud. Does it read easily and smoothly? If so, you are finished with your major revision work and are ready to indicate your sources formally.

STEP 9 PREPARE FOOTNOTES AND BIBLIOGRAPHY

How to Do Footnotes

Footnotes tell the reader the sources (book, articles, and other publications) of the borrowed material in the paper. Whether you quote directly or summarize ideas in your own words, you must acknowledge your sources through footnotes. In your early drafts, you indicated in parentheses the source and page number for borrowed information. Now, replace the material in parentheses by footnotes, which are introduced by numbers (1, 2, 3, etc.) elevated a half space and placed directly after the borrowed material.*

---

* In this chapter, the most traditional method of footnoting has been used. However, various disciplines have their own style manuals and the mechanics for giving sources may differ. You should, then, check with your instructors to see if they require a particular style.

Look at the model footnote entries on page 175. Footnote format differs depending on whether you use a book or magazine, whether there are one or two authors, and so on. Use the model entries when you prepare different kinds of footnotes. Pay special attention to spacing, punctuation, use of parentheses, and the order of the author's name.

The sample research paper illustrates the way footnotes are used at the bottom of a page to indicate the source for an idea. Note that a short ruled line separates the footnotes from the text. An alternative method (placing all footnotes on a separate "FOOTNOTES" page at the close of a paper) is illustrated on page 181.

How to Do a Bibliography

The bibliography is a list of the sources used in your research.* The bibliography makes it possible for a reader to go to one spot in the paper for full information about the works you consulted.

The last page of the model research paper (page 181) illustrates the correct format for a bibliography. Note the following points:

- The word *bibliography* should be in capitals and centered. Three spaces should follow before the first entry.
- The bibliography is organized alphabetically according to the author's last name.
- Entries without an author should be listed alphabetically by the first word in the title. Do not use the articles *A, An, The* when deciding how to alphabetize.
- Single-space each line of an entry; double-space between entries. Do not number entries.

Note the model bibliography entries on page 176. Bibliography format differs depending on whether you use a book or magazine, whether there are one or two authors, and so on. Use these entries as guides when you prepare your own bibliography. Pay special attention to punctuation, use of parentheses, and the order of the author's name.

---

* Bibliography format may vary from subject to subject. Check with your instructors to see whether they require a special format.

STEP 10 ASSEMBLE THE FINAL PAPER

Here are the guidelines to follow when you put together the final paper:

- Use good quality 8½ × 11 inch paper to type the final draft. Put items in this order: title page, outline, text, footnotes, and bibliography.

- Prepare a title page which has these items: the title of your paper (in capital letters and centered), your name, the name of your instructor, the title of the course, the date. There are many ways to display this information. See the title page (page 177) for the model research paper.

- Put your final outline on a separate page. Type the word "OUTLINE" in capital letters two or three inches down from the top of the paper. Then follow the format used for the outline (page 178) in the model research paper.

- Number consecutively each page in the paper except the title page. Page one is numbered at the bottom; numbers after the first page are put in the upper right-hand corner.

- Center the paper's title in capital letters on the first page of the text. Put the title two or three inches from the top and leave about an inch between it and the text. Do not underline the title.

- Leave margins of at least an inch on all sides.

- Double-space the text.

- Single-space and indent at the paragraph margin direct quotations of four lines or more. Use a double space to separate the quotation from the text that precedes and follows it. Do *not* use quotation marks around these long quotations (see page 180 for an illustration).

- Use brackets ([ ]) to show material added to a quotation. Use ellipses (. . .) to show material omitted from a quotation. See page 180 for illustrations.

- Proofread the paper carefully. Check for typing errors, omitted footnotes, words left out, and so on.

MODEL FOOTNOTE ENTRIES

Book by one author
    [1] Jerry Mander, Four Arguments for the Elimination of Television (New York: William Morrow and Company, 1978), p. 56.

Book by two authors
    [2] Richard Corriere and Joseph Hart, Psychological Fitness (New York: Harcourt Brace Jovanovich, 1979), p. 169.

Magazine article
    [3] Lynn Langway, "The Great Soda War," Newsweek, May 28, 1979, p. 75.

Newspaper article
    [4] Edward B. Fiske, "Toys Can Polish Preschool Skills," The New York Times, February 20, 1979, p. C1.

Encyclopedia article
    [5] "Scorpion," Encyclopaedia Britannica, 11th ed., XXV, p. 29.

Selection in an edited collection
    [6] Thomas Fox, "Fear Stalks the Elderly," in Ronald Gross (ed.), The New Old: Struggling for Decent Aging (New York: Anchor Books, 1978), p. 38.

Revised or later edition
    [7] Morris Hein, Foundations of College Chemistry, 4th ed. (Encino, California: Dickenson Publishing Company, 1977), p. 238.

> *Note:* The abbreviations *Rev. ed., 2d ed., 3d ed.,* and so on are also placed right after the title and separated from it by a comma.

Pamphlet
    [8] Theodore Irwin. How Weather and Climate Affect You, Pamphlet No. 533 (New York: The Public Affairs Committee, 1976), p. 42.

Television program
    [9] Dan Rather, "Mugged!" 60 Minutes, CBS-TV, February 25, 1979.

Film
    [10] Superman, Directed by Richard Donner, Warner Communications, 1978.

Recording
    [11] Barry Manilow, "Daybreak," in Greatest Hits, Arista Records, A2L-8601.

Interview
    [12] Dr. Joanna Walters, Personal interview on medicine as a career. Glassboro, New Jersey, March 30, 1979.

Second and later references to a work already cited
    [13] Mander, p. 72.

MODEL BIBLIOGRAPHY ENTRIES

Book by one author
Mander, Jerry. Four Arguments for the Elimination of Television. New York:
William Morrow and Company, 1978.

Book by two authors
Corriere, Richard, and Joseph Hart. Psychological Fitness. New York: Harcourt
Brace Jovanovich, 1979.

Magazine article
Langway, Lynn. "The Great Soda War." Newsweek, May 28, 1979, pp. 75–76.

Newspaper article
Fiske, Edward B. "Toys Can Polish Preschool Skills." The New York Times,
February 20, 1979, pp. C1; C4.

Encyclopedia article
"Scorpion." Encyclopaedia Britannica, 11th ed., XXV, 28–30.

> *Note:* No author is given for the above article. Do include the author's name in
> signed articles.

Selection in an edited collection
Fox, Thomas, "Fear Stalks the Elderly." In Ronald Gross (ed.). The New Old:
Struggling for Decent Aging. New York: Anchor Books, 1978.

Revised or later edition
Hein, Morris. Foundations of College Chemistry. 4th ed. Encino, California:
Dickenson Publishing Company, 1977.

> *Note:* The abbreviations *Rev. ed., 2d ed., 3d ed.,* and so on are also placed right
> after the title and separated from it by a period.

Pamphlet
Irwin, Theodore. How Weather and Climate Affect You. Pamphlet No. 533.
New York: Public Affairs Committee, 1976.

Television program
Rather, Dan. "Mugged!" 60 Minutes. CBS-TV, February 25, 1979.

Film
Superman. Directed by Richard Donner. Warner Communications, 1978.

Recording
Manilow, Barry. "Daybreak." In Greatest Hits, Arista Records, A2L-8601,
1978.

Interview
Walters, Dr. Joanna. Personal interview on medicine as a career. Glassboro,
New Jersey, March 30, 1979.

PAGES FROM MODEL RESEARCH PAPER

Title Page

THE THREAT TO MEDICAL CONFIDENTIALITY

by

David Blair

Professor Roberta Sandler
Sociology 101, Section 3
January 17, 1980

Outline Page

```
                            OUTLINE


Thesis:  Real concern has developed about potential abuses in the
         collection and storing of confidential medical information
         in centralized data banks.


  I.  Introduction
      A.  Pervasiveness of computer technology
      B.  Distrust of computers
      C.  Fear of private medical information being computerized:
          three issues of particular concern

 II.  First issue:  Questionable methods used to gather medical
      information
      A.  Transfer of information among corporations
          1.  Medical Information Bureau
          2.  Other information exchange systems
      B.  Private investigating agencies
          1.  Unprofessional practices
          2.  Inadequately regulated:  limitations of 1970 Fair Credit
              Reporting Act
      C.  Release or waiver forms signed by individuals
          1.  Anything but informed consent
          2.  Examples of releases with misleading wording

III.  Second issue:  Use of medical information for nonmedical purposes
      A.  No real control over the distribution of data
          1.  Inadequate technological monitoring
          2.  Informal distribution of information
      B.  Misuse of confidential medical data
          1.  Employers
          2.  Social agencies
          3.  Police

 IV.  Third issue:  Problem of individuals' access to their own records
      A.  Controversy about whether people care or not
          1.  The opinion of some representatives from health insurance
              industry
          2.  Dr. Rosen's study
      B.  Difficulties people face reviewing and correcting their records
          1.  Limitations of the legal right to gain access
          2.  Problems people have had with the Medical Information Bureau
      C.  Movement to guarantee citizens' right of access and correction
          1.  Freedom of Information Act (1974)
          2.  Privacy Act (1974)
          3.  Linowes' Privacy Protection Commission Report (1977)
      D.  More action needed
          1.  State and local level
          2.  Private sector

  V.  Conclusion
      A.  Real problems exist
      B.  What must be done to balance right to privacy with need for
          information
```

First Page of Text

THE THREAT TO MEDICAL CONFIDENTIALITY

Introductory paragraph

We live in a society where computers are everywhere. So accustomed have we become to computer technology that having computers in our home-- in such forms as minicalculators and video cassette games--does not seem unusual to us. Computer technology and its many benefits used to be greeted in this country with unqualified enthusiasm. More recently, however, there has been a growing fear that computer technology, if not controlled, may compromise basic human values. One of the most striking examples of this distrust of computerized systems is found in the area of

Thesis statement

medical record keeping. Real concern has developed about potential abuses in the collection and storing of confidential medical information in

Plan of development

centralized data banks. The following three issues in particular are receiving a good deal of attention: the questionable methods used to collect medical data, the use of medical information for nonmedical purposes, and the problems people have gaining access to their own centrally stored medical records.

Few people deny that confidential medical information is needed to process insurance forms, detect fraudulent claims, and plan for comprehensive health care programs and research projects.[1] What is protested, however, are the ways this information is collected. First of all, it is a common practice for companies to pool confidential medical information

---

[1] Allan F. Westin, _Computers, Health Records, and Citizens' Rights_ (Washington, D.C.: U.S. Government Printing Office, 1976), p. xii.

1

Second Page of Text

about individuals. David Linowes, Chairman of the U.S. Privacy Protection

Study Commission, emphasizes how widespread and dangerous this phenomenon is:

> Much of it $\underline{/}$ the medical information $\underline{/}$ is being shared with others
> without the knowledge of the individual concerned. With split-
> second retrieval, anything that is ever recorded about a person
> immediately becomes available; and with computer-to-computer linkage,
> anything put into the data bank of one organization can be tied
> together with another organization's data bank. This linkage . . .
> has the potential for creating one of the greatest threats to the
> privacy of the individual and eventually to our way of life.[2]

As the realization grows that confidentiality is being compromised,

organizations like the Medical Information Bureau (MIB) are increasingly

. . . .

---

[2]David Linowes, "Are New Privacy Laws Needed?" Vital Speeches,
May 1, 1978, p. 436.

Last Page of Text

15

Concluding paragraph

In summary, there are real problems regarding the use and misuse of

private medical records stored in computer banks. Moreover, given the

inevitability of some kind of national health insurance program, more

private medical information will no doubt be collected and stored in the

future. When that happens, Westin believes, people will feel even more

"uncertain and fearful about their capacities to control the circulation

of their medical and health data."[24] Right now, there are only haphazard

and difficult-to-enforce guidelines to regulate the collection and use of

confidential information. Westin believes that a combination of legislative

policy, judicial action, public debate, and consumer awareness will be

needed to balance the individual's right to medical privacy with industry

and government's need for health data.[25] Because the issues at stake are

so complex and significant, this kind of comprehensive attack is needed.

Without such an effort, The Privacy Report states, "the myth of medical

privacy will remain just that--only a myth, without substance."[26]

---

[24]Westin, p. 245.

[25]Westin, p. xviii

[26]The Privacy Report (New York: American Civil Liberties Union
Foundation, November 1977), p. 8.

Footnotes Page (if footnotes collected at end)

16

FOOTNOTES

[1]Allan F. Westin, Computers, Health Records, and Citizens' Rights (Washington, D.C.: U.S. Government Printing Office, 1976), p. xii.

[2]David Linowes, "Are New Privacy Laws Needed?" Vital Speeches, May 1, 1978, p. 436.

. . . .

[24]Westin, p. 245.

[25]Westin, p. xviii.

[26]The Privacy Report (New York: American Civil Liberties Union Foundation, November 1977), p. 8.

Bibliography Page

BIBLIOGRAPHY

Britton, Ann H. "Rights to Privacy in Medical Records." The Journal of Legal Medicine. July/August 1975, pp. 30-37.

"Health Records and Privacy: What Would Hippocrates Say?" Science. October 28, 1977, p. 382.

Linowes, David. "Are New Privacy Laws Needed?" Vital Speeches. May 1, 1978, pp. 436-439.

McClellan, Grant S., ed. The Right to Privacy. New York: The H.W. Wilson Company, 1976.

The Privacy Report. New York: American Civil Liberties Union Foundation, November 1977.

Reutter, Mark. "Private Medical Records Aren't So Secret." The Baltimore Sunday Sun, July 13, 1975, pp. 1-4.

Tolchin, Martin. "Carter Maps Policy to Protect Privacy." The New York Times, April 3, 1979, pp. 1; 17.

Westin, Allan F. Computers, Health Records, and Citizens' Rights. Washington, D.C.: U.S. Government Printing Office, 1976.

Activities

1   Review the chapter carefully. Then, without looking back, answer the following questions.

1. After you select a general research area, you must then decide how to _____ the topic.

2. True or False: _____ Some research papers make and defend a point of some kind; others simply present information about a particular subject.

3. When taking notes, you should:
   a. Use 3 × 5 or 4 × 6 inch cards.
   b. Write on one side only.
   c. Put only one kind of information on any one card.
   d. All of the above.

4. Notes that you take for your research paper may be in the form of:
   a. Direct quotation   c. Combination of the two
   b. Summary in your own words   d. All of the above

5. You are _____ if you fail to acknowledge that you have used someone else's idea in your paper.

6. One way to organize your note cards is to write at the top of each card a _____ that summarizes the content of the card.

7. True or false: _____ You must credit a source even if the information you present is common knowledge.

8. The central idea of a research paper is known as its:
   a. Thesis statement   c. Topic sentence
   b. Plan of development   d. Working purpose

9. _____ are numbers (1, 2, 3, etc.) elevated a half space and placed directly after borrowed material.

10. True or false: _____ When writing a bibliography entry, reverse the order of the author's first and last names.

2 Writing footnote entries On a separate sheet of paper, convert
the information in each of the following references into correct footnote form. Use the appropriate model on page 175 as a guide.

1. A reference to page 75 of *Final Payments,* a novel by Mary
   Gordon published in New York by Ballantine Books in 1979.

2. A reference to page 40 of an article by Thomas J. Cottle titled
   "Adolescent Voices" in the February 1979 issue of *Psychology
   Today.*

3. A reference to page 73 of an article by Jane Bryant Quinn
   titled "A Woman's Place" in the February 26, 1979 issue of
   Newsweek.

4. A reference to page 127 of an article by John Dewey titled
   "Education as Growth" in the book, *The Open Classroom Reader,*
   edited by Charles E. Silberman and published in New York
   by Random House in 1973.

3 Writing bibliography entries On a separate sheet of paper, convert the information in each of the following references into correct
bibliography form. Use the appropriate model on page 176 as your
guide.

1. A book by Ellen Goodman called *Turning Points,* published in
   New York by Doubleday and Company in 1979.

2. An article by James Daniel titled "Seven Shelters Against
   Inflation" on pages 109–113 of the March 1979 *Reader's Digest.*

3. A book by Jerome Kagan and Ernest Havemann called *Psychology: An Introduction* published in a third edition in New York
   by Harcourt Brace Jovanovich in 1976.

4. An article by Richard Schickel titled "Woody Allen Comes of
   Age" on pages 62–65 of the April 30, 1979 *Time.*

Answers

Note: Some questions are open-ended. Answers are not given in those cases where more than one response is possible.

1 DOING WELL IN COLLEGE

Activities (page 9)
1. d
2. False
3. c
4. They say the following:
   a. "I can't do it."
   b. "I'm too busy."
   c. "I'm too tired."
   d. "I'll do it later."
   e. "I'm bored with the subject."
   f. "I'm here and that's what counts."
5. False
6. d
7. Placement office
8. d
9. Counseling center
10. False

2 MANAGING YOUR TIME

Question (page 13): 15 class hours
22 study hours

Question (page 14): 15 separate blocks
3 different benefits

Question (page 15): Sunday evening

Question (page 15): Monday (4:00–5:00)
Tuesday (9:00–10:00)
Wednesday (10:00–bedtime)
Thursday (3:00–4:00)
Sunday (10:00–bedtime)

Question (page 15): The question about Rich rewarding himself with a free day is a matter of individual choice. Many people feel it is a good idea to have a full day's break in a busy weekly schedule. On the other hand, keep in mind that if you are so busy on occasion that you need Saturday study time to keep up with your work, you should not hesitate to take the time.

Question (page 16): In one of his three study periods on Thursday.

Question (page 16): Morning study hours

Question (page 16): Saturday evening

Question (page 16): Sunday morning or later Sunday evening

Activity 2 (page 21)
1. Exam dates and paper deadlines
2. b, d, and f
3. b
4. d
5. c

3 TAKING AND STUDYING CLASSROOM NOTES

Activity 2 (page 33)
1. 80 percent; write down
2. e
3. c
4. Indenting; skipping
5. True

Activity 3 (page 34)
Suggested key words:

5 sources of truth
Def and ex of intuition
Def of authority
2 kinds of authority
2 kinds of secular authority
Limit of scientific authority

(*Note: Definition* and *example* have been abbreviated; *authority* and *scientific* could have been abbreviated.)

Activity 5 (page 36)
1. They lose attention when listening to a speaker.
2. 125 WPM talking; 500 WPM listening
3. a. Summarize what the speaker has said
   b. Try to guess where the speaker is going next
   c. Question the truth and validity of the speaker's words
4. Intend to listen carefully

Activity 6 (page 39)
1. The rumor, the fad or fashion, the craze, and mass hysteria
2. A rapidly spreading report not supported by proven fact
3. To support belief and to satisfy the desire for gossip
4. "Streaking"; pet rocks; fashions in clothing such as the unisex clothing of recent years
5. A craze often becomes an obsession for its followers. A fad is trivial; a craze can become a very serious matter.
6. Some form of irrational, compulsive belief or behavior which spreads among people.
7. Students at a Louisiana high school were seized by an uncontrollable twitching that spread like wildfire; rash of flying saucer reports

Activity 7 (page 43)
1. Biological, safety, social, esteem, self-actualization, cognitive, aesthetic
2. Food (*or* hunger), water, air, sex drives
3. The institution of the family; wanting jobs with security; saving money for emergencies; purchasing insurance policies
4. Need to belong to a group and to give and receive love
5. By achieving personally meaningful goals
6. Need to become what one is capable of becoming; need to live up to one's potential
7. Cognitive needs
8. An appreciation of the beautiful

4   READING AND STUDYING TEXTBOOKS I: TWO STUDY SYSTEMS

Activity 1 (page 57)
1. c
2. Numbers
3. True
4. d
5. d

Activity 6 (page 62)
The Importance of Attention
Attention is important because it helps us learn.

Factors That Influence Attention:
1. Motivation—powerful aid to paying attention. By relating the subject matter being studied to our own motives, we can sharpen our attention.
2. Feedback—information on how well the learning process is going. Feedback helps us correct our mistakes (e.g., feedback while typing) and holds our attention by providing evidence that learning is taking place.

    Programmed learning—contents of a course are broken down into very small steps. Students get immediate feedback on their learning.
3. Rewards—two kinds:
    a. External—extrinsic; come from the outside. E.g., children are rewarded with gold stars or candy, college students with good grades. Rewards are, in a sense, bribes—effective ones.

        In one study, a psychologist successfully helped "uneducable" boys learn by providing a reward system.
    b. Internal—intrinsic; inward feelings of personal satisfaction; pleasure of learning for sake of learning.

        E.g., children learn to ride bike for rewards of achievement and sense of power.

        Internal rewards are more effective aids to attention than external ones.

5 READING AND STUDYING TEXBOOKS II: KEY READING SKILLS

Activity 1 (page 73)
1. True
2. Def; Ex
3. e
4. a and c
5. Heading

Activity 2: Locating Definitions and Examples (page 73)
1. Territoriality—persons' assumptions that they have exclusive rights to certain geographic areas, even if these areas are not theirs by legal right.
    Ex—after first week of class, students consider a certain seat to be their territory.

    Personal space—space surrounding our body, a space that moves with us.
    Ex—persons in a public reading room seek at least one empty space between themselves and next reader.
2. Energy—the capacity to do work.

    Potential energy—stored-up energy or energy an object possesses due to its relative position.
    Ex—water behind a dam.

    Kinetic energy—energy that matter possesses due to its motion.
    Ex—water behind a dam allowed to flow.
3. Positive transfer—what I have learned to do well in one situation applies equally well in another situation.
    Ex—frequent joke telling works well in one class so teacher tries it in another.

    Negative transfer—what worked in one situation was not applicable to another situation.
    Ex—frequent joke telling does not work well in talk at faculty club.

Activity 4 (page 75)
1. Two Basic Forms of Immaturity
    1. Fixation—person remains emotionally at an earlier level of development
    2. Regression—return to an earlier level of maturity
2. Accomplishments of 1966 Congress
    1. Created the Dept. of Transportation
    2. Passed a $1.2 billion "demonstration cities" program
    3. Established safety standards for all highway vehicles
    4. Broadened the regulations for the labeling and packaging of foods, drugs, cosmetics, and household supplies
    5. Appropriated $3.7 billion to help clean up the country's rivers and lakes and $186 million to fight air pollution

3. Steps in Solving a Complex Problem
   1. Identify the problem
   2. Search for possible solutions
   3. Analyze the situation
   4. Move to the attack itself

Activity 6 (page 76)
The War of 1812
1. What caused the War of 1812?
2. How long did the war last?
3. What countries were involved?
4. Who won the war?

The Dark Ages and the Glimmer of Light
1. When were the Dark Ages?
2. What was the glimmer of light in the Dark Ages?

Taft-Hartley Act
1. What is the Taft-Hartley Act?
2. When was it passed?
3. What were its values and drawbacks?

Coping with Frustration
1. What are ways of coping with frustration?
2. What are the effects of not coping?
3. What kind of person seems to do the best job of coping with frustration?

The Social Dropouts
1. Who were the social dropouts?
2. Why did they become dropouts?
3. What are ways of preventing people from dropping out?

Heredity and Development
1. What is heredity?
2. How does heredity affect development?
3. Is heredity as important as environment in affecting development?

Pollution and Business
1. How does business contribute to pollution?
2. How can pollution by business be regulated?
3. How serious and widespread is pollution by business?

Characteristics of Living Things
1. What are the characteristics of living things?
2. What is the most basic characteristic of living things?

The Two Terms of Theodore Roosevelt
1. Why was Roosevelt elected to a second term?
2. What were the achievements of Roosevelt's two terms?
3. What were the failures of Roosevelt's two terms?

Heart Disease
1. What is heart disease?
2. What causes heart disease?
3. How can heart disease be **prevented or controlled?**

Activity 7 (page 77)
1. Three professional economists **appointed by the President and approved by** the Senate
2. Thinking and investigating
   Thinking
3. President Kennedy
   To teach and work with **native citizens of a country in any way that would** be of help
   (*Note:* The political **purpose of creating the Peace Corps was to win back** some of the friends of the United States who had been alienated by the Bay of Pigs invasion.)

Activity 10 (page 79)

Emphasis	*Addition*
most important	moreover
most significant	also
especially valuable	another

Illustration	*Change-of-direction*
for example	but
for instance	yet
such as	however

Activity 11 (page 79)
1. Oldest and most persistent (emphasis)
   For instance (illustration)
   But (change-of-direction)
   Also (addition)
2. For example (illustration)
   Also (addition)
   Moreover (addition)
   More important (emphasis)
3. Major goal (emphasis)
   However (change-of-direction)
   Another (addition)
   For example (illustration)

Activity 12 (page 80)
1. b
2. d
3. a

Activity 13 (page 81)
1. During the Depression, money shortages produced important changes in the daily lives of people.
2. When purchasing toys, parents should resist the impulse to buy something which appeals to them and concentrate on buying toys that are suitable for the child.
3. In short, the human body needs sleep to function, much as it needs food and water.

6   TRAINING YOUR MEMORY

Activity 1 (page 90)
1. Organize
2. b
3. False
4. Intend
5. Hooks

Activity 2 (page 90)
Here is one possible set of groups:

Daily newspaper	Kent cigarettes
Reader's Digest	Muriel cigars
Newsweek	Bic lighter
Dental floss	Tide detergent
Colgate toothpaste	Dial soap
Toothbrush	Joy dish detergent
Scope mouthwash	Ban deodorant

Activity 3 (page 90)
One possible catch word in RIDE.

7   TAKING OBJECTIVE AND ESSAY EXAMS

Activity 1 (page 111)
Following directions: _____   DAVIS, SUSAN

Matching: 1. e   *Davis, Susan*
2. g
3. a
4. c
5. d
6. f

Fill-ins: 1. study
2. first
3. most important
4. budget

True or false: 1. True
2. True
3. False
4. False

Multiple choice: 1. c
2. b
3. d
4. d

Activity 3 (page 114)
1. *c. Hint.* Answer in the middle with the most words is usually correct.
2. b. *Hint:* If two answers have the opposite meaning, one is probably correct.
3. e. *Hint:* The first answer and the other answers may be correct, in which case the correct response is "all of the above."
4. False. *Hint:* Answers with absolute words are usually false.
5. True. *Hint:* Rework questions that contain double negatives.
6. True. *Hint:* Answers with qualifying words are usually correct.

8   WRITING EFFECTIVE PAPERS

Activity (page 132)
1. Point
2. d
3. Support
4. True
5. Process
6. Thesis statement
7. b
8. Outline
9. Narrow
10. True

9   DOING A SUMMARY

Activity 1 (page 139)
1. True
2. d
3. a
4. Subtitle or caption
5. Preface

10   PREPARING A REPORT

Activity 1 (page 148)
1. Reaction
2. False
3. d
4. Introduction; conclusion
5. Support

11 USING THE LIBRARY

Activity 1 (page 158)
1. b
2. d
3. Call number
4. c
5. True

Activity 2 (page 158)
1. Among books by John Kenneth Galbraith:
   The Affluent Society   *A China Passage*
   The Age of Uncertainty   *The New Individual State*
   American Capitalism
2. Among books by Betty Friedan:
   The Feminine Mystique   *It Changed My Life*
3. Pearl Buck
4. Claude Brown
5. Many books are possible.
6. Many books are possible.
7. *Silent Spring*
   - Rachel Carson
   - Boston
   - Houghton Mifflin
   - 1962
   - (1) Pesticides—Toxicology; (2) Wildlife Conservation; (3) Insects, injurious and beneficial—Biological control
   - SB959/C3

   The Hidden Persuaders
   - Vance Packard
   - New York
   - David McKay and Company
   - 1957
   - (1) Advertising—Psychological Aspects; (2) Propaganda
   - Hf5822/P3

   The Immense Journey
   - Loren C. Eisley
   - New York
   - Random House
   - 1963
   - (1) Man—Origin; (2) Evolution
   - QH368/E38
8. *Note:* Books other than those listed below may be given.
   Abraham Maslow
   - *Toward a Psychology of Being*
   - Princeton, New Jersey

- Van Nostrand
- 1962
- (1) Personality; (2) Motivation (Psychology)
- BF698/M338

Margaret Mead
- *Growing Up in New Guinea*
- New York
- William Morrow and Company
- 1930
- (1) Manus tribe; (2) Children in New Guinea; (3) Education of Children
- GN671/N5M4

David Riesman
- *The Lonely Crowd*
- New Haven
- Yale University Press
- 1950
- (1) National Characteristics—American; (2) Ethnopsychology
- BF755/A5R5

Activity 3 (page 159)
1. Nathaniel Hawthorne
2. World War II
3. Women
4. Russia
5. Mathematics

12 WRITING THE RESEARCH PAPER

Activity 1 (page 182)

1. Limit (*or* narrow)	6. Heading (*or* label)
2. True	7. False
3. d	8. a
4. d	9. Footnotes
5. plagiarizing	10. True

Activity 2 (page 183)

[1] Mary Gordon, Final Payments (New York: Ballantine Books, 1979), p. 75.

[2] Thomas J. Cottle, "Adolescent Voices," Psychology Today (February 1979), p. 40.

[3] Jane Bryant Quinn, "A Woman's Place," Newsweek (February 26, 1979), p. 73.

[4] John Dewey, "Education as Growth," in Charles E. Silberman (ed.), The Open Classroom Reader (New York: Random House, 1973), p. 127.

Activity 3 (page 183)

Goodman, Ellen. Turning Points. New York: Doubleday and Company, 1979.

Daniel, James. "Seven Shelters Against Inflation." Reader's Digest, March 1979, pp. 109–113.

Kagan, Jerome, and Ernest Havemann. Psychology: An Introduction. 3d ed. New York: Harcourt Brace Jovanovich, 1976.

Schickel, Richard. "Woody Allen Comes of Age." Time, April 30, 1979, pp. 62–65.

Acknowledgments

J. Jeffrey Auer: *Brigance's Speech Communication,* 3d ed., p. 32. Copyright © 1967. Reprinted by permission of Prentice-Hall, Inc., Englewood Cliffs, N.J. Selection 2 on page 77.

Frank J. Bruno: From *Psychology: A Life-Centered Approach.* Copyright © 1974 by John W. Wiley and Sons, Inc. Selection 1 on page 80.

James C. Coleman and Constance L. Hammen: From *Contemporary Psychology and Effective Behavior.* Copyright © 1974 by Scott, Foresman and Company. Reprinted by permission. Selection on page 68.

Frank D. Cox: Adapted from *Psychology,* 2d ed. Copyright © 1973 by William C. Brown Company. Reprinted by permission. Selection 2 on page 82.

Paul R. Ehrlich, Richard W. Holm, and Irene L. Brown: Adapted from *Biology and Society.* Copyright © 1976 by McGraw-Hill, Inc. Reprinted by permission. Selection 3 on page 81; Selection on page 86; Selection on page 124.

Stanley K. Fitch: Adapted from *Insights into Human Behavior,* 2d ed. Copyright © 1974 by Holdbrook Press, Inc. Reprinted by permission. Selection on page 73.

Norman A. Graebner, Gilbert C. Fite, and Philip L. White: From *A History of the American People.* Copyright © 1975 by McGraw-Hill, Inc. Reprinted by permission. Selection on page 70; Selection 3 on page 75; Selection 3 on page 82.

Morris Hein: From *Foundations of College Chemistry,* 4th ed. Copyright © 1977 by Wadsworth, Inc. Reprinted by permission of the publisher, Brooks/Cole Publishing Company, Monterey, Calif. Selection 2 on page 74; Selection 2 on page 79.

Richard Hofstadter, William Miller, Daniel Aaron, Winthrop D. Jordan, and Leon F. Litwack: Adapted from *The United States,* 4th ed. Copyright © 1976 by Prentice-Hall, Inc. Reprinted by permission. Selection on pages 71–72.

Paul B. Horton and Chester L. Hunt: Adapted from *Sociology,* 4th ed. Copyright © 1976 by McGraw-Hill, Inc. Reprinted by permission. Selection on pages 34–35; Selection on pages 37–39; Selection on pages 48–49; Selection on pages 65–66.

Elizabeth B. Hurlock: Adapted from *Adolescent Development,* 4th ed. Copyright © 1973 by McGraw-Hill, Inc. Reprinted by permission. Selection on pages 108–109; Selection on page 122.

Edward B. Johns, Wilfred C. Sutton, and Barbara A. Cooley: Adapted from *Health for Effective Living,* 6th ed. Copyright © 1975 by McGraw-Hill, Inc. Reprinted by permission. Selection 1 on page 79.

Kenneth Jones, Louis W. Shainberg, and Curtis O. Byer: From *Dimensions,* 2d ed. Copyright © 1974 by Harper and Row. Reprinted by permission. Selection 1 on page 75.

Jerome Kagan and Ernest Havemann: Slightly abridged and adapted from *Psychology: An Introduction,* 3d ed. Copyright © 1976 by Harcourt Brace Jovanovich, Inc. Reprinted by permission of the publisher. Selection on pages 59–61.

Robert Kelley: From *The Shaping of the American Past.* Copyright © 1975 by Prentice-Hall, Inc. Reprinted by permission. Selection 2 on page 80.

David Kretch, Richard S. Crutchfield, and Norman Livson, with the collaboration of William A. Wilson, Jr.: From *Elements of Psychology,* 3d ed. Copyright © 1974 by Alfred A. Knopf, Inc. Reprinted by permission. Selection on page 73.

Clifford T. Morgan and Richard A. King: Adapted from *Introduction to Psychology,* 5th ed. Copyright © 1975 by McGraw-Hill, Inc. Reprinted by permission. Selection 3 on page 74; Selection 3 on page 79.

Charles G. Morris: Adapted from *Psychology: An Introduction,* 2d ed. Copyright © 1976 by Prentice-Hall, Inc. Reprinted by permission. Selection on page 72; Selection 3 on page 75; Selection 3 on page 82.

Gerald D. Nash: Adapted from *The Great Transition.* Copyright © 1971 by Allyn and Bacon, Inc. Reprinted by permission. Selection 3 on page 77; Selection on page 120.

Jerry B. Poe: Adapted from *An Introduction to the American Business Enterprise,* 3d ed., pp. 3–5. Copyright © 1976 by Richard D. Irwin, Inc., Homewood, Ill. Selection on page 31; Selection 1 on page 77.

Index